D1018625

# CRISIS OF FAITH

# CRISIS OF FAITH

*Second Edition Revised and Enlarged*

Thomas Keating, O.C.S.O.

ST. BEDE'S PUBLICATIONS
Petersham, Massachusetts

*Ecclesiastical permission received from*

+Bernard J. Flanagan
*Bishop of Worcester*

*June 29, 1970*

Quotations from the Gospels are reprinted with the permission of the Bruce Publishing Company from **The New Testament** by Kleist and Lilly. Copyright 1956. Quotations from the Old Testament from the translation by Monsignor Ronald Knox, Sheed and Ward, Inc., Copyright 1950.

LIBRARY OF CONGRESS CATALOGING IN PUBLICATION DATA

Keating, Thomas.
  Crisis of faith.

  1. Christian life—Catholic authors.   2. Bible. N.T. Gospels—Meditations.   I. Title.
BX2350.2.K39   1979          248'.48'2          79-13036
ISBN 0-932506-06-2
ISBN 0-932506-05-4 (paper)

Second Edition, Revised and Enlarged
Second Printing, June 1982
Third Printing, December 1986
Fourth Printing, March 1989

# Contents

| | | |
|---|---|---|
| I | The Crisis of Faith | 1 |
| II | Examples of Faith | 7 |
| III | A Crisis of Growth | 13 |
| IV | The Canaanite Woman | 18 |
| V | The Silence of Jesus | 24 |
| VI | Time Was Made for Waiting | 28 |
| VII | Lazarus | 34 |
| VIII | Martha and Mary | 41 |
| IX | The Goal of the Crisis of Faith | 44 |
| X | The Grace of Mary Magdalen | 50 |
| XI | The Sources of Praise | 56 |
| XII | The Greater Grace of John | 61 |
| XIII | The Absence of Jesus | 68 |
| XIV | The Patience of Job | 73 |
| XV | The Widow's Mite | 80 |
| XVI | The Reward of the Widow's Mite | 83 |
| XVII | PETER: The Formation of a Disciple | 88 |
| XVIII | LAZARUS: Symbol of Christian Awakening | 117 |

# I. The Crisis of Faith

Pentecost is the feast of spiritual maturity. Few really relish this feast or even have much idea of what it is all about. It presupposes a lot. Some theology, some knowledge of the liturgy, but mostly personal experience.

There is an analogy between growing up spiritually and the growing up that takes place in the normal course of human life. In approaching adolescence and adulthood, everyone seems to have to pass through a crisis. Extraordinary changes take place around the time of puberty when a child is about to become an adolescent. Even greater changes occur in adolescents as they approach maturity.

Our Lord told us very clearly that, however mature we may be naturally, to enter the Kingdom of God we have to become like little children. There is then a law of growth in the life of grace.

Consider the picnic beside the Lake of Tiberias.[1] It is one of those incidents, of which there are many in the period between Easter and Pentecost, in which we are meant to see the disciples of the Lord coming of age. In their case, they had the privilege of telescoping a lot of experience into a few days or weeks. They seem to pass from infancy to spiritual maturity in fifty days. No doubt there was good reason in their case for such an accelerated course. But experience seems to indicate that after the time of that first Pentecost, it takes the best of Christians closer to fifty years.

In this scene we see Simon Peter gently repulsed. It was

his custom to treat Our Lord in a rather free and easy manner. Here he leaps out of the boat, swims to the shore, and comes running up to Our Lord dripping wet. I do not know what he expected to hear or receive, but he is told quietly to take it easy. There is no hurry. Breakfast is under control . . . "Go and get a couple of the fish out of the big haul." And so he goes to help the others who have brought the boat to shore and are counting up the fish—one hundred fifty-three in all. It must have taken quite a while to count them.

An aura of mystery fills this scene. No one dares ask the mysterious Person, "Who are you?" knowing that it is the Lord. They are overawed by His presence. It begins to dawn on them that something is different. They have to keep in the background and let the Lord do what He wants. It is up to Him to take the initiative. Their human way of dealing with Him, the sensible relationship on which they had depended, is coming to an end; and they do not know quite what to do. They have not learned as yet any other way of communicating with Him.

Finally He calls them: "Come and have breakfast."

They all sit down around the campfire He has prepared for them. He knew how weary they were after the long night. There is every evidence of loving concern on His part. And yet it is not the same. They cannot talk with Him as freely as before. That is the note which we are left with: a distinct change is taking place in the relationship of the disciples with the Master.

The same kind of experience happened to Mary Magdalen in the cemetery when Jesus appeared to her after His resurrection.[2] She threw herself at His feet—or was it into His arms? When this had gone on for a while, Jesus said, "Well now, stop clinging to me! Don't you realize that I am risen from the dead? There is something different about our relationship now. I am about to ascend to my Father and to your Father. Go and tell this to the disciples."

The former warm human relationship, something she has been used to, is over. Gently He brings her around to realize that there is something different. She must forge a new relationship with Him based on the new degree of spiritual growth which His resurrection has bestowed upon her and which His ascension is about to complete.

Finally there is Thomas who questioned the fact of Our Lord's resurrection.[3] After seeing the risen Jesus in the flesh, he heard these paradoxical words addressed to him: "You would have been far better off not to have seen me and to have believed! You would have been so much happier! You would have grown up so much if only you had accepted my resurrection inwardly on faith rather than outwardly on the basis of a presence you can see and touch."

What took place in the souls of the disciples during those fifty days between Easter and Pentecost is taking place in us. At some point in our spiritual growth Jesus asks us to adjust ourselves to a new relationship with Himself. Since this happens without much warning, almost no one has any awareness of what is taking place when it actually happens. It comes on gradually, slowly but surely. However, we can so successfully distract ourselves from our interior life that we actually never make the adjustment and never forge the new relationship Jesus asks of us. The whole process can sort of drop out of our attention. Some people who have received a distinct gift for prayer lose it, because at the time of this transition they surrender to excessive activity, get fed up, or stumble over some obstacle to forging the new relationship.

One has to forge new relationships not only with Jesus, but with other people. Most of us form dependencies on the external side of the spiritual life. This often involves a great dependency on some *one*. He may be the superior or novice master, or pastor, or a much appreciated and loved confessor or spiritual director. But along comes this inevitable transition from childhood to adolescence, the moment described in the Gospel incidents just mentioned. We may fail to make the transition successfully through our own blindness and inability to accept good direction, through the lack of any guidance at all, or because of bad advice.

Sometimes someone in this painful and perplexing situation, feeling great dryness and consequently under considerable strain, is urged to distract himself in order to ease the anguish of searching for Christ in the darkness of faith. This is a great mistake. A spiritual director should distinguish between somebody who is really under a strain through natural causes, and someone who is going through this crisis in his spiritual development and whom the Divine Action is pulverizing. If such persons are urged to take things too easy, they may lack the courage to face this transition. If only they would persevere in prayer, they would pass into a new freedom and liberty. Such a victory can only be bought at a great price, the death of something: the death in this case of a superficial and self-centered spiritual life and its relationships.

How often someone who has a wonderful relationship with a superior, pastor or spiritual director runs into some misunderstanding or other. Perhaps he is entrusted with some position where he is expected, and has to have, a judgment of his own. He begins to see a situation differently from the superior, the pastor, or his spiritual director, and he gets into a row. All of a sudden the man looks different. He appears in all his human rags and tatters. It almost seems as if he were acting improperly—something is wrong with his moral theology or sense of social justice. And there is a crash! And this person thinks the wonderful relationship has come to a complete end.

What needs to be done here is simply to realize that the old relationship has indeed come to an end; that God wants it to come to an end; and that He wants us to climb up to a new relationship based on a new growth, on a new maturity. If there was great dependency on someone, that has to be changed. A new relationship must be forged, one less dependent, one more worthy of one's new growth and maturity. On the basis of this new growth all the facets of one's life must progress. This is a great struggle. Sometimes it may seem impossible. God inspires us, if we are faithful to grace, to work it out.

Unfortunately, quite a few people do not work it out, but turn—there is no other word for it—sour. They get bitter about the whole thing. It is the old problem of the umbilical cord on the psychological plane. They feel something is wrong when they start growing up. It was so nice and warm in the womb of mother. And it was so nice and warm in the old relationship, be it sensible consolation from Christ, be it a wonderful understanding with the superior, or be it that consolation and encouragement that we had from our spiritual director.

Our Lord has great sympathy for those who are going through this crisis in their spiritual life. They do not know what is happening to them and tend to concentrate on the disintegration of what they love, rather than on the real spiritual growth of which they are becoming capable.

There are tragic situations where someone instead of

growing up, makes up his mind that everybody else is wrong. Because of all that they have received they stand a greater risk than anyone else of really getting God angry. That can happen if they decide to become permanently bitter and sour at the moment when this transition is suggested to them. This is probably what happened to Judas. He refused to grow up; he refused to pass on to a new and deeper relationship with Christ.

Growing up is a great opportunity in spite of its hazards. If we look on the bright side and are firmly convinced that it is normal to have to forge these new relationships, our crisis of faith will appear as a great invitation to go deeper into the Heart of Christ. The very transition makes it impossible for the former people we counted on to help us. Part of growing up is to become independent—not of everybody, but of those on whom we are too dependent— so that we may depend completely on the Holy Spirit. That is what spiritual maturity is.

[1]John 21:1-14
[2]John 20:11-18
[3]John 20:19-25

## II. Examples of Faith

The new principle of life won for us by Christ's passion, death and resurrection, is dynamic and hence must grow and come to maturity. We must give it room to grow.

This new life is not superimposed on our natural powers like a penthouse on a lovely apartment house. Quite the contrary. For this new life to grow, it has to make use of the place where the old building is standing. This involves a mammoth demolition project, or at the very least, a thorough top-to-bottom renovation.

Suppose you had a piece of property on Wall Street with an old dilapidated tenement standing on it. It would be too expensive to buy a new piece of property and build a new building alongside the old. You would remove the old building and put the new one in its place.

Now we have only one small plot in the whole of creation over which God has given us full control and responsibility, that is, our own being. There is room for only one building: the one we have constructed, or the one God wants to construct. We must choose.

The crisis that we are speaking about is not limited to one or two events. Like coming to adolescence or adulthood, there are a series of experiences, one building on the other, and the whole producing a new and stable level of life.

There are two great crises in the process of spiritual maturity. The centers of gravitation around which these two crises revolve are faith and love. Of course, the theological virtues are organically connected—growth in one is a growth in the others. It is rather a question of emphasis. The emphasis in the first crisis is on the growth, purification, and strengthening of faith; in the second, on the growth, purification, and deepening of love.

For the present let us consider only the first crisis, that of faith. In John's Gospel we have the following scene:[1]

Our Lord was on His way to Cana. Along came a royal official from Capernaum, pleading, "Come down and heal my son!"

Our Lord showed great reluctance to go, saying, "Unless you see striking signs of power, you do not believe."

But the man cried out in desperation, "Sir, come down now. My son is on the point of death!"

Jesus replied, "You go. Your son is healed." The man went down and at the same hour—the Gospel is careful to bring that point out—the very moment Our Lord uttered the words, the fever left the boy.

Another scene.[2] This time it was at Capernaum. Along came a centurion and said to Jesus, "My slave is sick and is suffering frightfully."

Jesus said, "I will come down right away and heal him."

The centurion objected, "Oh no! Just say the word and my servant will be healed. I am unworthy that you should come under my roof."

In these two instances we see Our Lord adjusting Himself to men possessing different degrees of faith. The first man believed in the power of Our Lord's presence. His weak faith required the physical presence of Jesus. He did not apparently believe that Jesus could heal his little son without coming down and physically laying His hands upon him. He is a symbol of those who need to feel the sensible presence of Our Lord, at least from time to time, to sustain their faith.

And what does Jesus do? He refuses to go down.

Why? Because the absence of His physical presence is to be the occasion of increasing this man's faith. When the royal official went back to Capernaum believing in Our Lord's word and found that everything was as Jesus had said, then he came to believe in the power of His word alone. I repeat, the absence of the felt presence of Our Lord is His normal means of increasing our faith and of getting us to the point of believing in the power of His word alone, without "signs and wonders," that is to say, without the feeling of His presence or external props.

It is a crisis of faith that He puts the royal official through, and with great success. From that time on, he believed. In fact, his whole household got the benefit of his growth in faith.

The centurion had a greater degree of faith. He already believed in the power of Our Lord's word alone. That is why Our Lord was quite willing to go with him. Jesus showed Himself most accommodating. This gave the centurion the opportunity of manifesting his high degree of faith.

Our Lord was astonished and delighted with this manifestation of faith. "I haven't found such faith in all Israel!" He cried out.

Then He said to the centurion: "My dear friend, since you believe, you can have anything you want."

Our Lord reveals His secrets in the ins and outs of these two Gospel narratives. They are worth studying carefully. He wants very much to give us His gifts, but our weakness and our individual psychology requires that He proceed with caution, with a certain diplomacy. He can only give us what we are capable of receiving at the present moment. The events that He allows or causes to happen, if we respond with faith, give Him the chance to increase our faith. He did not go down to the bedside of the royal official's son because the man needed to have his faith increased before Jesus could put Himself, so to speak, at the disposal of his desires.

We are not much different from our friends in the Gospel. Each of us is more or less a problem to Our Lord. He responds to us according to the degree of faith which we have right now.

The crisis of faith does not just revolve around our relationship with Our Lord, it revolves around all our relationships. With our neighbor, our boss, those we are trying to help.

Take a concrete example. Here we have someone in the same spiritual state as the royal official. He has great faith in Our Lord, great courage in the service of God, an exemplary Christian; but only so long as he is sustained, not by faith alone in Our Lord's word, but by consoling experiences. He gets a little hopped up once in a while at the liturgy over some feast or other, especially if the hymns are well sung.

Our Lord says to Himself: "I think this person has been long enough in the stage of infancy. Let's see if he can exercise his muscles a little bit and those legs of his and walk on his own feet." And so, He removes His consoling presence.

At this same time there may be someone who is a great help to this good soul, but too much so. And Our Lord asks Himself, "I wonder how much this lad is really serving Me, or how much he is just relying on this other guy? Does he really put his faith in Me? Well, I think I'll find out."

He may cause a little rift. By way of example, let us consider a crisis of obedience in the life of a young religious. The superior asks him to do something which interferes with the little program of sensible consolations that he has lined up for himself. He wants peace and quiet and that requires a job with no responsibility whatsoever. So along comes this assignment that threatens his little plan. And so he cries out to Our Lord: "My little nest is threatened! Come down and save me."

But Our Lord replies, "Unless you have all those consolations, I doubt if you would serve Me. I doubt if your faith would hold up."

He cries out louder and louder, "Come down! Come down!"

Jesus answers, "I'll take care of the situation without coming. Just believe that everything is all right and that I am handling the situation, and go your way in peace."

Then he is presented with this dilemma: "Shall I believe Our Lord? Shall I base myself on His word, or not?" That is the crisis.

There is not just one of them. There are a whole series cf them, one right after the other. Out of the first ten, he may miss eight. Fortunately God keeps asking, keeps returning, keeps leading him on like a father his little son whom he is trying to teach to walk. He takes a few steps, falls down, gets up and takes a few more.

How many have the courage and faith of this royal official, and as soon as Our Lord says, "Well now, that's the end of all of these sensible consolations and props," turn around, square their shoulders, and walk right back to Capernaum?

One more incident which exemplifies again the way God works, this time in the case of those very close to Him. I am thinking of the family of Bethany that Jesus loved so much. Lazarus had fallen desperately sick and Mary and Martha sent Jesus a message saying: "Please, Lord, your dear friend is ill."[3]

Lazarus was actually close to death and the two sisters wanted him very much to be cured. Yet they did not really ask for anything. They just laid the problem before Him. They believed in the power of Our Lord's physical presence. They evidently believed too in the power of His word alone, because they didn't ask Him to make the trip. He was busy and they did not want to bother Him. All they wanted to do was say: "Here's the problem. You handle it."

The Gospel says, "Now Jesus loved Martha and Mary and Lazarus." But the next sentence has a strange ring to it: "When He heard, therefore, that Lazarus was sick, He tarried there two days."

A plan was forming in the back of His mind. He knew He could trust these special friends. He recognized in this event a good occasion to raise their faith and love to new heights. Perhaps He had been waiting for this occasion for a long time. He knew they desperately wanted Him to come. He loved them. And yet, "He tarried there two days,"—that is, He *ignored* them for two days.

If Our Lord loves you very much, do not expect that He is going to be on the job the moment that you have need of Him. On the contrary, He appears not to be on the job. But He is on the job more than you think. He has things all planned in the back of His mind. He feigns disinterest. He ignores you for the moment. But that is the surest sign of something really wonderful about to happen. When Jesus finally came to Bethany, He raised Lazarus from the dead.

[1]John 4:46-54        [2]Mt. 8:5-13        [3]John 11:1-44

## III. A Crisis of Growth

The Gospels tell us both in plain language and through symbolic events how the life of grace which we have received in Baptism grows up from infancy to adulthood. The cure of the son of the royal official and the cure of the centurion's servant are two examples of this symbolic method of teaching. They show us the dispositions of two people with different degrees of faith and how Our Lord dealt with them according to the degree of faith which each one possessed. Let us look at the incidents again.

The story of the cure of the son of the royal official opens with these words: "He came again to Cana in Galilee, where He had changed the water into wine."

That introduces still another incident—the changing of water into wine.[1] What was the event, and why does John mention the first miracle of Our Lord, as he recounts the second?

If you recall that incident, there was a problem over the wine at the wedding feast. The wine was running out and Mary, the Mother of Jesus, was concerned about it. She spoke to Our Lord and after some hesitation He finally relented and changed an enormous amount of water into wine.

This is a most symbolic incident in John's Gospel and the point of departure for all the other miracles. According to St. Augustine,[2] the water symbolized the Old Law, and the wine the New. The Gospel is the new wine, the grace of

Christ, which has come to us at the request of the Mother of Jesus.

Now the changing of water into wine is not the changing of water into better water. It is the changing of one substance into another, into something quite different. And that is precisely the point of this second miracle, and why John recalls the first one. What actually happened in this incident is that a man is really changed from something he was, which was not too good, into something quite new, which was very good. Christ has come, the miracle of Cana tells us, to transform us—the human creature into the divine, water into wine, something lesser into something greater—at the price of ceasing to be what we were before.

"So He came again to Cana in Galilee, where He had changed the water into wine."[3] Now we are given a picture of the son of a certain royal official who is lying in bed in Capernaum with a high fever. His anxious father, hearing that Jesus had come from Judea to Galilee, goes out to meet Jesus and begs Him to come down and heal his little boy, whom he believed to be on the point of death.

"If you do not see striking exhibitions of power," Jesus said to him, "you will not believe." This was certainly a rebuke. There is a great deal of irony in those words, "exhibitions of power." You almost get the impression that Our Lord really despises His own miracles. They are the dreadful necessity for people who just will not come around and believe as they should. At this time, there is unquestionably in the back of His mind the plan of changing this man's weak faith into something new, something living, something strong. It is a rebuff, there is no doubt about that. Our Lord underlines exactly what is wrong with this man's petition: it lacks faith.

But Jesus, by seeming to repulse his request, increases his desire. And so the man pleads, "Come down, Sir, before my child dies!"

At this Jesus assures him, "Go, your son is safe and sound."

"The man had faith in the word Jesus had spoken and went his way." It had not occurred to him before that moment that Our Lord could actually heal his son without being there.

The withdrawal of Our Lord's felt presence is meant to increase our faith, and without the withdrawal of that sensible presence we cannot but remain on this very weak, watery level exemplified by the royal official.

I wonder what this man was thinking about while he was returning home. He had faith in Our Lord's word for the first time in his life. Up to that moment he had confidence only in the power of Jesus as man. Perhaps he had heard about the miracle of Cana. Now he was beginning to have faith in the power of this man as God, because only God can work a miracle at a distance. He had only had faith in the power of Jesus' physical presence. Now he had faith in His omnipresence. He believed in His divinity.

But faith in the divinity of Jesus is attained at the price of the loss of His physical presence. We can well imagine that on his way home—it was a long walk and a hot day—he remembered his son lying in bed the way he had left him. Many a distressing thought must have crowded in upon him, "Can it really be so? Is he really cured?" Imagine the quickening of his steps and of his heartbeat as he approached the town.

When he met his servants, they said, "Yesterday..." It was a long walk! It was a long night in which he hung on to faith in this Person whom he had come to believe was God.

The Mother of Jesus had told the waiters at the wedding feast of Cana, "Do whatever He tells you." This man was carrying out the same injunction. The result was that his faith was changed from water into wine.

He was still on the road when his servants met him; no doubt they were running to meet him. They called out to him, "Your son is safe and sound!"

What a moment that must have been for this poor man! He experienced the inward leap which comes to everyone who realizes that he has passed through a profound spiritual crisis successfully. He had struggled, believed, hoped. It was a long and painful trial, but suddenly it is taken away. Everything is okay. He made it! And the inward satisfaction comes, one which is superior to any other kind of satisfaction: the joy of knowing that he wound up, perhaps for the first time in his life, on God's side.

The Gospels are rightly compared to wine. They contain real joys which leap up inwardly in one's inmost being like the sweetness of wine, or even like the exhilaration of too much wine.

In the thrill of having believed and of having found out that his hope was not misplaced, a flood of relief swept over the royal official. He was convinced that Jesus was really God. His whole family believed. His own faith bubbled over on everybody else at home. No doubt there was a great deal of rejoicing, of hugging and kissing and weeping.

"This is the second time that Jesus gave proof of His claims after returning from Judea to Galilee."

And what was the first time? The first time was when He

materially changed water into wine. This time He effects
what the former miracle signified. He transforms a man's
weak faith into a strong living faith. But only at the price
of a crisis, at the price of death to his own desires and judgment. The physical presence of the Master which he
wanted, and which he thought he needed, had first to be
taken away.

In our own spiritual growing up process we cannot
escape the crisis of faith. This incident clearly teaches us
that it is not merely a rebuke when Jesus seems to push us
against the wall and to remove the props which we feel are
so necessary for us. It is rather a call to new growth, to the
transformation of our weakness. It is a call to a new union
with Him, a call to "launch out into the deep."[4]

The great pity is that we so often fail to meet this
challenge. We bog down in our demands for Christ's felt
presence or for other props to our faith. If we would allow
them to go and believe in His word alone, in His divinity,
we would then experience that transformation of our faith,
the fruit of which is a new outpouring of the Holy Spirit,
symbolized in John's Gospel by the wine. Remember that
the Holy Spirit is a spirit. He cannot be attained by means
of feelings or reasoning. By allowing the former kind of
relationship to be taken away—or to be torn away—we
make it possible for Him to transform our faith into an
abiding awareness of God.

[1]John 2:1-11
[2]Homilies on St. John, Tract XLIX
[3]John 4:46-54
[4]Luke 5:4

## IV. The Canaanite Woman

By refusing the request of the royal official to go to heal his son, Our Lord gave him the opportunity to rise to a higher degree of faith. The centurion was a man in almost exactly the same outward situation as the royal official. He also had someone, his slave, whom he wanted cured. Instead of refusing to go down, Jesus showed Himself most willing and eager to oblige. He did this in order to give the centurion the opportunity to manifest the magnificent faith he had in the power of His word alone. It also gave Our Lord the opportunity to bring that extraordinary faith to the attention of His disciples.

Now let us take a look at somebody who had even greater faith. And this, I think, will bring us even closer to the meaning and purpose of the crisis of faith.

Our Lord had just withdrawn into the neighborhood of Tyre and Sidon, a country outside the confines of Israel. Out of that district came a Canaanite woman.[1] She was a gentile. At this time of sacred history, gentiles had no right to the privileges of the children of Israel. But somehow or other she had found faith in Christ, and as the story unfolds, she exercised it to a most extraordinary degree.

She pleaded with Him, "Have pity on me, Master, Son of David!" (This Messianic reference indicates that she believed in Him as the Messiah.) "My daughter is sorely tempted by a demon."

"But in answer to her request He did not say a word."

Certainly not much of a reply! At least the other two people got an answer. This woman gets nothing.

The greater your faith, the slower may be the reply to your prayers. The Lord knows He can take His time with you and busies Himself with other, less fortunate people—although at such a time you may feel yourself to be the most unfortunate of all.

Evidently she did not let His apparent refusal bother her much, because she next appeals to the disciples. She chose some intercessors for herself, and with considerable success, because the disciples took up her cause with the Lord saying: "Let her go home contented, she cries so after us."

This reminds one of those elderly ladies one finds, or at least used to find, in almost every large parish church, who go visiting all the statues at the side altars, appealing to St. Joseph, St. Jude and St. Everybody. And I dare say that in heaven the same cry goes up from the saints, "For heaven's sake, give this lady what she wants and let us have some peace!"

However, I am not applying this text to eschatological events. I am trying to uncover the dispositions of a soul who is appealing to Our Lord with faith and receiving only silence in reply. Notice, it is not only silence, but coldness. His reply to the disciples was, "My mission is exclusively to the lost sheep of the house of Israel."

In other words, "Nothing doing."

It is not so very different from the reply our Blessed Mother received at the wedding of Cana. The wine was running out. A very embarrassing situation was developing fast. She laid the necessity of these newlyweds before Our Lord. But He protested, "My hour is not yet come."[2] In other words, apparent refusal.

Our Blessed Mother accepted it fully, but at the same time she did not hesitate to say quietly to the waiters, "In case He should change His mind, be sure to do whatever He says."

The Canaanite woman evidently had a similar faith. She understood Our Lord to say "no" as clearly as our Blessed Mother did; but "she herself came and prostrated herself." She understood Him to mean "no" on one level, but she thought, "Perhaps if I get down on a lower level, I can get a new hearing."

So she prostrated. She got all the way down, completely flat, so that she could go no lower.

Here are her words: "Master, help me!"

Who, even you and I, as hardhearted as we are, would not have said, "There, there, it's not so bad. Maybe I can do something for you after all."

But, "He *demurred*." Still no apparent sign of pity, mercy, human kindness. He just said, "No!"

This poor creature has received as an answer to her prayer only silence, coldness, refusal.

Now comes rebuff. "It is not fair," He said, "to take the children's bread and throw it to dogs."

Here is a woman completely spread out at His feet, in a position which Our Lord takes full cognizance of, because He says He does not want to take the bread and throw it on the floor where she is lying waiting to receive it. If that is not a stinging rebuff to a simple, straightforward human appeal, I do not know what more you want.

Our Lord knows the material with which He is dealing. He is dealing with a woman of extraordinary dispositions. Gradually He leads her on from one peak of faith to another. But notice His means: silence, coldness, rebuff, humiliation.

What is her reply to this indignity?

She said, "You are right, Master." She accepts the humiliation. "You are dead right, there is no question about it. It would be wrong to take the children's bread and throw it to dogs. No argument whatsoever. I agree with you wholeheartedly."

And then comes one of those answers which the Holy Spirit inspires, one of those marvelous distinctions which comes from no human wisdom however elevated. It is one of those fine distinctions that only love can come up with. After having fully accepted the humiliation, her position there on the ground, and His apparent refusal, here is her reply: "It is true, everything you say, dear Lord. But how about this? The dogs eat the crumbs that fall from their master's table."

In other words, "I'm not asking for food which I deserve. For I acknowledge that I deserve none. I have no merits of my own. But after the children have eaten, aren't there always a few crumbs left over? How about dropping me some of these? And not some that you throw to me, but some that just fall by accident off the table? And here I am down on the floor. Maybe I can catch one. What do you say?"

This woman unquestionably fathomed the strange conduct of Our Lord towards her. She was not a Jew. She had no instruction except from the Holy Spirit. But with His help she completely conquered the Heart of Jesus.

The text reads, "Jesus *acquiesced.*" He was beaten at His own game. But with great pleasure, because He cried out in delight, "O woman, great is your faith! . . . you can have *anything* you want!"

This heroic act of faith was what Our Lord was waiting for. Had He acceded right away, granted her petition at

the first or second request, she would never have risen to
these heights. There is no way to spiritual maturity, to
growth in faith, except by this road.

Who is this daughter who was so "sorely tempted by a
demon?" It might not be too farfetched to consider the
daughter as a symbol of what Paul calls "the physical part
of our being,"[3] which is truly tormented by a demon at this
crisis in our lives when we go to Our Lord, and His former
tenderness, sweetness, and whatever else we may have
received, are turned to dust and ashes. The more we plead,
the less we seem to be heard. The lower we crawl in the
dust, the more He seems to suggest getting lower. It is the
cry from a heart that is really serving God which Our Lord
seems to turn down here. Why? Because we are "un-
profitable servants" and have no right to "the food of the
children." We have no true right to anything in the order
of grace. It is precisely by facing up to this reality that we
pass from confidence in our own merits to faith in His
mercy. As soon as she acknowledged that she had no right
to the food, she got not only a crumb, but the whole
banquet. That is really the substance of the crisis of faith—
and it's resolution.

How many can take those long weeks, months, and perhaps years of praying and apparently receiving nothing?
First we are driven to our knees, then to our hands and
knees, then down on our stomachs with our faces in the
dust. How many can go through this without wavering in
the hope that God is going to answer their prayers, give
them control over their rebellious human nature, and
establish them in union with Christ?

The Canaanite woman had the kind of faith which penetrates the clouds. She would not take any kind of refusal as
a real refusal, as a real "no." She kept on praying with

faith. The more she was tried, the more she placed her trust in Jesus, until she finally achieved her goal and got all she wanted.

This is the disposition God waits for in the crisis of faith: trust in His mercy no matter what kind of treatment He gives you. Only great faith can penetrate those apparent rebuffs, comprehend the Love which inspires them, and totally surrender to It.

[1]Mt. 15:21-28
[2]John 2:4
[3]2 Cor. 4:16

## V.  The Silence of Jesus

I would like to review once again the dialogue between Our Lord and the Canaanite woman to bring out another aspect of the crisis of faith. The question to be answered is: what constitutes successful passage through the crisis of faith? This determined woman, I think you will agree, successfully passed through her crisis in a few moments. It will doubtless take us many months or years to negotiate ours.

She came out of the district of Canaan crying, "Have pity on me, Son of David, because my daughter is sorely tormented by a demon!" Now the Gospel says, "In answer to her, Jesus replied not a word."

Let us observe these words rather closely. You will notice the Gospel does not say He gave no response. Nor does it say He answered "yes" or "no," but simply: "In answer to her request, He did not say a word."

In other words, as far as Our Lord was concerned, silence, lack of response, is a real answer. In this particular case it is the answer that the woman got to her request.

As we listen carefully to this exchange between Our Lord and the Canaanite woman, we observe a gradual change in her dispositions. And that change marvelously illumines what the passage through the crisis of faith is meant to lead to in our relationship with God.

Let us translate this incident into our own everyday experience. Here is someone whom Our Lord is trying to draw away from a childish and self-centered relationship with Himself to something more mature and worthy of God. This person has faith, but it is still very weak, based in large part on the experience of effort and success. We have a way of looking at all our activity and judging it on the basis of success: so much so that if we put in effort and fail to get proportionate results, we feel frustrated. Suppose we do some good spiritual reading and put in an hour of prayer every day, or spend a year or two studying Theology or Scripture. We expect to see some fruit. If we think of fruit in terms of spiritual progress which we can feel and understand, we are in for a great disappointment. As time goes on, the more effort we make to get closer to Jesus, the more He seems to recede into the recesses of the books or of the tabernacle. He always seems to be "out" when we call.

Now this is exactly the situation that the Canaanite woman found herself in. She went to Our Lord and asked Him, with faith, for the same kind of favor that He had shown Himself most willing to grant to other people. His reply to her was *silence*. But *silence* is a very real answer to prayer.

Let us look at the dialogue a little further. She started working on the disciples. They finally came to Jesus and complained, "Lord, for goodness sake, send this lady home contented, she cries so after us. She gives us no peace."

Here again the answer is not "yes" or "no." It is the rather enigmatic statement: "My mission is exclusively to the lost sheep of the house of Israel."

Finally she came and prostrated herself before Him. Notice that the delay, if anything, is increasing her desires. It also seems to be increasing her humility. Having prostrated, she pleads, "Master, help me!"

The reply again is not "yes" or "no," but another enigmatic statement: "It isn't fair to take the bread of the children and throw it to dogs."

This is an abstract or speculative statement. In the speculative order, it is not fair to help her. He appeals to the fact that His food rightly belongs to the people of His household, not to slaves, and still less to dogs, to which category He implies that she belongs. In other words she has no right to any help. But that is not to say that she is not going to get any.

There is just a hint in these words that Our Lord's defenses are breaking down. "That isn't fair" is a rather weak argument people often make when they are about to give in. It represents their last stand. Perhaps she sensed this in her extraordinary wisdom. In any case, with great pleasure she accepted the insult—without, however, withdrawing her request. It was not a clear refusal, otherwise she would have been disobeying Our Lord. If He had said "no," she would not have been acting rightly. But He did not say "no." The answers He is giving her, while they appear to be refusals, are actually a series of come-ons, of invitations to hope.

Her faith in this dialogue gradually blossoms into confidence. She penetrates somehow into the mysterious silence of Our Lord. She recognizes His enigmatic refusals to mean merely delayed action. Not a brush off, but a postponement. The postponement in granting her request is the occasion He takes to raise her, by means of His secret grace, from faith, to hope, to confidence. There is no real confidence which is not based on the struggle to be patient in suffering and the experience of God's help.

When faith grows into confidence, the crisis of faith has

done its work and the crisis itself is resolved. Deep interior peace reigns.

The Lord does hear. The silence of Jesus is the ordinary means He uses to awaken in us that perfect confidence which leads to humility and love—and to gaining all that we ask.

Ask somebody whom Our Lord is trying to jockey into this kind of crisis, and he usually will say something like this: "I'm going backwards. God doesn't love me anymore. He doesn't listen to my prayers. He never gives me what I want. I can't find Him in books. Prayer is a mess, one distraction after another. Temptations of every kind abound."

And yet underneath all that debris there is the same kind of perseverance and longing for contact with God which shows that grace is secretly at work. What is being destroyed is our dependence on our own ways of going to God. Actually these much loved souls are being invited by Christ to the same kind of expansion of faith that the Canaanite woman experienced. Remember what the grand finale was. At a certain point, when her confidence reached the degree Our Lord was waiting for, He acquiesced and said to her, "Woman, great is your faith. You can have anything you want!"

What we really want and what the Holy Spirit is inspiring us to long for in the crisis of faith is a confrontation with the Word of God in our inmost being. It is contact with the Divinity of Christ. It is to be brought inwardly face to face with the living God, Who, faith assures us, dwells within us, and Who, hope reassures us, will reward those who seek Him with His presence.

## VI.  Time Was Made for Waiting

The spiritual progress revealed in the events which we have just reviewed is not a kind of growth that we can feel and understand. The values involved in spiritual growth are quite different from the values indicating progress in some other sphere, such as running a business, taking higher studies, or learning a trade. If you are making headway in these things, you experience greater facility, satisfaction, possession of skill. These natural indicators of progress are pretty much the reverse when it comes to spiritual matters. This is illustrated very well in the incident of the Canaanite woman.

She came forward to speak to Our Lord with reasonable self-assurance. She knew of His kindness and compassion. She had heard of many people He had helped. She had heard of His miracles and believed in them and in Him. She did not anticipate any difficulty in obtaining her request. It was a well deserving and humble request. She spoke to Our Lord in a way that she had heard other people had done. She is a good example of those who have reached a certain degree of faith and expect that things will continue to remain the same forever.

There comes, then, this mysterious *silence*. Call it aridity, dryness, desolation, whatever you want. The terrible, inner realization grows that no matter how hard we try, or how loud we cry, there is not going to be any response from the other side of eternity.

We tend to make judgments according to the way we

feel. Until we have passed through the crisis of faith, there is not much understanding of Our Lord and His ways. We tend to judge Him as we would anybody else who seemed to be ignoring us. And so the judgment forms in our hearts: "He doesn't love me anymore!" After all, if you try to talk to someone and he constantly turns around and walks away, the logical conclusion is, "There is not much use in keeping this thing up. It's a little too one-sided. God pays no attention to me. Therefore He does not love me."

Now the precise purpose of the crisis of faith is to free us from the prejudice of our feelings so that we can make judgments and act according to faith and reason.

Suppose we take the Israelites, the children of God's household, to whom the food belongs by right, as examples of those who feel they deserve a certain amount of attention from God on account of their good works. Generally, when you have given up a great deal for God or have served Him energetically for a while, you start feeling virtuous. You may have taught catechism for a few months or attended daily Mass for a few years. Maybe you refrained from hitting someone in the face when he insulted you. So everybody in your little world begins to think that you are really the cat's whiskers. "Here is somebody who really practices his religion," they say.

If you are good at arguing, you may convince someone that he should go to church or get back to the sacraments. Maybe you even succeeded in converting some poor devil. You begin to feel as though God owes you something. Really you are quite a virtuous person. At least other people think so, so why contradict the obvious?

We generally expect people to think well of us and are not surprised when some morsel of praise comes our way. And from that it is a short step to think that God thinks the same about us. He more or less relies on us to keep the world going and the Catholic Church as it should be.

Then one day we come to make our request like the Canaanite woman and there is no reply. We begin to wonder whether we have done something wrong. Am I going backwards? Not at all. The first step, you might almost say, the first sign of movement, as far as getting anywhere in the spiritual life, is to begin to be anxious about whether we really are such good friends with God. I do not say this should be a terrible anxiety, but it should shake the foundations from under our colossal self-satisfaction. It does not cross our minds that we desperately need help until the innumerable props on which we have been relying begin to crumble.

The first reply that Our Lord gave the Canaanite woman, or rather the coldness that He showed her, brought her down a little more. For her next request, she prostrated. He was gradually pulling the carpet out from under her. He finally had her down on the ground with her nose in the dust. It took her a short time to reach that point but, let's be frank, it is taking us quite a few years.

As a matter of fact, most of us are not really convinced of original sin, especially when things are going well. We spend a few years being kind to people, a few years without temptations of the flesh, and we think all our troubles are over. We have passed to angelic life and will never more experience movements of anger or sensuality. In other words, there is no original sin. But there *is* original sin, and it is so real that to ignore it, practically speaking, is not to be humble. Humility consists in accepting the whole of reality, and original sin is at least half of it.

When Our Lord by His passion and death gave us back grace, He did not give us back integrity, that is to say, the

perfect control of our lower nature by reason and will—
that was the gift that He gave Adam. Maybe you would
like to pick a bone with Our Lord for not giving it back.
The only trouble with that is that we are just the clay and
He is the potter. There is no use saying, "Look here, why
didn't you complete the job? You did so much. You could
have done one little thing more. You could have restored
our fallen human nature to what it was before."

But He did not do so. And He did not do so because it
was His will to show the power of His grace in our fallen
human nature. He may also have wished to make sure that
no human being would again make the same mistake that
Adam made, which was to presume, through lack of
experience of human weakness, on the gifts of God.

Although Our Lord by His passion and death has raised
us to a much greater supernatural height and dignity than
we had when Adam was the father of the human race, He
has left our nature fully in the appalling weakness, blindness, and ignorance to which it fell through original sin. It
is the triumph of Christ's passion when the Holy Spirit
places the tiny seed of grace in this pile of rotting manure,
which is the way it sometimes feels, and causes that tiny
seed to grow and transform all the rubbish and debris into
a garden of paradise.

The grace of Christ will accomplish this if we bear
witness, through the experience of our weakness, to the
freedom and liberality of the Giver, and attribute all the
glory to Him. What God objects to, is for a man to come
along and say: "I had something to do with this. Look
what I've done. Isn't it terrific!"

Spiritual progress consists first of all in embracing the
reality of original sin as it exists in ourselves, but without

despairing. That is difficult to do. Human nature is constantly presented with two great temptations: despair and pride. Everybody who likes to oversimplify and to solve things by the quick route, in three easy lessons, is very much tempted in one direction or the other. Either he gives the spiritual life up as impossible, "I'm too bad," which is a sin against hope. Or he says, "Well, I guess I'm pretty good after all with all these virtues of mine, I'm all set," and that is presumption.

Our Lord, in the scene with the Canaanite woman, gently but firmly, desiring only to lead her to union with Himself, brings her to face reality. He teaches her that she is nothing, and that she deserves nothing. He brings her to agree that she does not deserve the least consideration. He has her groveling there in the dust in front of Him. Yet through the power of His secret grace, she keeps on hoping in spite of the delay.

The habit of waiting for God gradually establishes us in a right attitude towards Him. We cannot push God around. But that is what we try to do when we say, "Give me this; give me that." Or even, "Please, give me this."

Some even make bold to say: "If you don't give me this, I won't say any more prayers."

Or, "How can you do this to me?"

But God's answer to all this is: "Well, who are you?"

There is nothing so humbling as waiting—that is why time was created, so that we might learn to wait. Waiting makes you feel inferior to the person who is keeping you waiting. And this begins to dawn on you the longer you have to wait. That is why some people cannot stand it any more and get up and walk out.

But God has the right to make us wait not only for an hour, or a day, or a week, or a month, but our whole lifetime. By waiting we come to accept the fact, as the Canaanite woman did, that God is the Lord; we are only a creature, and whatever we have is His pure gift. Although He wants immensely to give us supernatural gifts, He is not going to make the same mistake, if that is the word for it, that He made with Adam. He will not give them until we have fully learned, tasted, and accepted our lowliness and poverty.

Humility is the whole-hearted acceptance of the fact that God owes us nothing and that we owe Him everything. We must first learn to wait with patience. When we begin to wait with confidence, we are beginning to come out on the other side. By waiting long enough in the presence of the God whom we reverence as our Creator and Lord, we gradually find ourselves loving Him as our Father and Friend. Faith becomes more and more penetrated with love, and love understands God by means of habitual contact with Him.

## VII. Lazarus

By way of introduction to the next Gospel incident, we must take a quick look at an earlier event.[1] Our Lord had made friends with a family consisting of Lazarus and his two sisters, Martha and Mary. They lived in Bethany, a town near Jerusalem. Jesus seems to have made a point of stopping with them on His journeys to and from the Holy City.

Luke describes one such occasion during which Martha was busily preparing a meal for Jesus, "while Mary seated herself at His feet and listened to His words." Martha became a little vexed at her sister's neglect of the chores and rebuked her for her lack of solicitude about the success of the meal. Apparently Our Lord was not overly anxious about the dinner either, for He defended Mary's repose. In Mary we recognize a person whose faith has deepened through love and who is beginning to be absorbed, not so much by the words of Jesus, as by His person. She is beginning to penetrate the human nature of Christ and to lay hold of His Divinity.

Now let us turn to the dramatic event of the raising of Lazarus from the dead.[2] This incident puts before us an interesting comparison between the faith of Martha and Mary. Let us see how each one responds in the circumstances. Our Lord obviously makes use of this occasion to raise the faith and love of His friends to heights of personal commitment which they never would have attained otherwise.

It is the same with us. Some striking event, some crisis upsetting the ordinary run of things, may become the take-off point for the divine action. Our Lord waits for just the right moment to give us a special grace, to bring home to us our hidden motives, or to manifest to us (and to other people) our possession (or lack) of good dispositions. The spiritual life is a life, and therefore it can go in two directions. It can grow and it can decay.

Here we have Lazarus who is introduced as a close friend of Jesus. He falls sick, and within a few days dies. Jesus tells the disciples that he has only fallen asleep. Of course He knew He would raise him from the dead.

There are three people in the Gospel whom Jesus raised from the dead: Jairus' daughter, in her own home,[3] the son of the widow of Naim, on his way to the tomb,[4] and Lazarus, after he had been four days in the tomb.[5] As St. Augustine suggests,[6] we may understand by these three deaths symbols of three kinds of sin: secret sin, represented by the raising of Jairus' daughter in her home; public sin, represented by the raising of the poor lad who was being carried to the tomb; and habitual sin, represented by the raising of Lazarus who was not only dead, but rotting.

Now each one of these people was thoroughly dead. Death, we know from Scripture, is the penalty of sin and a symbol of spiritual death.

These three people then are symbols of those who have suffered spiritual death, and who, as far as the life of grace goes, are inwardly corpses in varying degrees of corruption.

A person who is spiritually dead cannot move unless Christ comes along and raises him from the dead. That is the tremendous meaning of the sacrament of Penance.

The three whom Our Lord raised are truly tragic

figures. Each one is a warning to us. Lazarus is the most striking warning of all because he is someone described by Our Lord as "our friend." He is a symbol of a baptized Christian who has fallen into habitual sin—one who is not only sick, but dead and corrupting—who is absolutely helpless unless Our Lord comes along and raises him from the tomb of spiritual death.

Let us push the symbol one step further in its poignancy. Lazarus is not only the symbol of a baptized Christian who has gone astray; he is the symbol of a religious, someone for whom Our Lord has shown special love, and whom He rightly calls His "friend." He is the symbol of a priest, in accordance with Our Lord's words at the Last Supper: "I shall not call you servants, but friends."[7]

Here is someone who is the symbol of a religious or a priest, or both, who has entered the crisis of faith and has begun to slip. First illness sets in and then death—sin. Then comes corruption—habitual sin. What kind of sins? Pride, avarice, envy, gluttony, vainglory, ambition, lust, and all the others. A religious or priest is no more exempt from these temptations than anybody else.

The two sisters send a message to Jesus full of resignation and faith. "Master, your dear friend is ill." They started their prayers for him when they saw that something was going wrong. Jesus said to the disciples, "This illness will not result in death, but is going to promote the glory of God. Through it the Son of God is to be glorified."

"Now Jesus loved Martha and her sister and Lazarus. So when He learned that he was ill, He tarried, it is true, for two days in the place where He was." John's words indicate a certain astonishment at Jesus' slowness in coming to the rescue.

At last Jesus suggests to the disciples that they go to Lazarus. It was a bad time for Him to appear anywhere near Jerusalem from the point of view of His mission, because the leaders of the Jews were out to get Him. The disciples did not like the idea at all, and they recommended against it. Our Lord then announced, "Lazarus, our friend, has fallen asleep. Well, then, I will go and wake him from his sleep."

St. Augustine has some interesting words on this point. He says: "Belief in Christ is Christ in our hearts, and the sleep of Christ in our hearts is the forgetfulness of faith." And so if our faith begins to get a bit sleepy, then comes this regressive process, illness and death.

When Jesus arrived at Bethany, He found that Lazarus had already been four days in the tomb. "Bethany was near Jerusalem and many of the Jews had called on Martha and Mary to express their sympathy with them in the loss of their brother."

Now notice the reaction of the two sisters. As soon as Martha heard that Jesus had arrived, she went out to meet Him, but Mary remained at home. Martha said to Jesus, "Master, if you had been here my brother would not have died, and now I know that whatever you ask of God, God will grant you."

Her faith was already expanding to the point where she was ready to believe that Jesus could raise him from the dead. She knew He could have prevented his death.

Our Lord said to her, "Your brother will rise again," asking her to believe in the resurrection of Lazarus. She rises to this new and great act of faith: "I firmly believe that you are the Messiah, the Son of God, Who has come into the world."

"With this she returned and called her sister, Mary, privately, 'The Master is here and asks for you.' As soon as Mary heard this, she rose quickly and went to meet Him."

Notice that Mary did not go right away. She did not go until she was sent for. Martha, however, with her usual eagerness to serve, dashed right out and put her petition before Our Lord. She accomplished nothing. Our Lord remained right where He was.

Mary waited until He sent for her. Why should she go out to seek Him whom she possessed within? She had that discretion which comes from deep love, a certain supernatural poise which does not put itself forward, but waits calmly for the moment of grace. But as soon as He sends for her, then she rises up promptly and hastens to meet Him. In every respect she shows herself to be the master of herself, not anticipating the invitation of God, not slow to obey, nor yet carried away by strong emotion, even by the call of Our Lord. She receives the grace of His visitation without losing her head.

Martha's overeagerness had accomplished nothing.

The Jews now all followed to see where Mary was going. She came and threw herself at Jesus' feet as soon as she saw Him, saying exactly the same words as Martha: "If you had been here, my brother would not have died." The same words, but notice that she gets the results. It is not words that count, but the motive which prompts them. Her greater faith and love obtain the miracle.

She was on her knees before Him. She started weeping. This was too much for Our Lord.

"She was weeping and weeping too were the Jews who accompanied her. The sight of them stirred Jesus deeply and shook His inmost soul."

"Where have you laid him to rest?" Jesus asked.

"Come and see, Master," they replied. Jesus burst into tears.

What was passing in the heart of Jesus? The Jews remarked, "Look how dearly He loved him."

But was it only for Lazarus He was weeping?

Some said: "He opened the eyes of the blind man, was He not able to prevent this man's death?"

This shallow reasoning with the implied judgment that He did not care much about Lazarus must have been extremely painful for Jesus to hear.

"Then Jesus, His inmost soul shaken again, made His way to the tomb." Upon reaching the place, He said, "Remove the stone. "

This command astounded the people who had followed Him. The body had been four days in the tomb with the stone rolled in front of it. Jesus is now asking Martha and Mary to believe that He can raise their brother from the dead. This is a bit too much for Martha. She has not quite reached this degree of faith. With her usual practical bent, she warns, "Master, his body stinks by this time. He has been dead four days."

But Mary says nothing. Her faith holds out. Remember that Lazarus is a symbol of someone who has been Christ's friend and for whom everybody has given up hope— except Mary. It is her faith that Jesus is actually counting on in order to work this miracle.

They start to roll back the stone. Out come odors of corruption. They hesitate.

Jesus insists: "Did I not tell you that if you have faith, you will see the glory of God?"

With trembling hands they take away the stone. Martha is trembling. Mary is silent. The eyes of all are fixed on Jesus.

"And He, lifting up His eyes, said, 'Father, I thank you for listening to me. For myself I know that you always hear me, but I said it for the sake of the people surrounding me, that they might believe that I am your ambassador.'

"And having said this, He cried out with a strong voice, 'Lazarus, come forth!'

"And he who had been dead *came* forth, wrapped hand and foot with bands, his face muffled with a scarf.

"And Jesus said, 'Loose him and let him go.' "

What was this strong cry if not the sign of God's love for the sinner, for one of His friends who had gone astray, who was dead and must be called back to Life?

[1]Luke 10:38-42
[2]John 11:1-44
[3]Luke 8:40-56; Mt. 9:18-26
[4]Luke 7:11-17
[5]John 11:1-44
[6]Homilies on St. John, Tract XLIX, 3
[7]John 15:15

## VIII. Martha and Mary

Our Lord frequently manifests very different reactions to what seem like identical requests. We saw how the royal official asked if He would please come down and heal his son, and Jesus refused to budge. When the centurion approached Him on behalf of his slave, He spontaneously offered to go with Him. The former needed faith; the latter had faith and proved it. It is to us, then, rather than to our requests, that Our Lord responds.

In the story of the resurrection of Lazarus, we observe Jesus reacting in a way that reminds us of His treatment of the royal official and the centurion. Martha goes to see Him and He remains outside the town. Mary does not go to see Him until sent for, and at her unspoken request He at once enters the town.

The text reads: "As soon as Martha heard that Jesus was coming, she went out to meet Him."[1]

In spite of Martha's request, He stayed right where He was. When Mary went out at Jesus' invitation and showed Him her tears, He was deeply moved and immediately came into the town and raised Lazarus from the tomb. The crisis of faith comes into focus right at this point. The purpose of the crisis of faith is to bring us to a radical willingness to live by faith alone and to give up the support of sensible consolations.

Here is the paradox illustrated by comparing the royal official and the centurion, and then Martha and Mary: seek Jesus' sensible presence—a consoling presence you can feel and understand—and you will not find Him. Give up seeking the consolation of His sensible presence, and you will find Him.

This idea is expressed by the text of Isaiah quoted in the Epistle to the Romans: "I was found by these who did not seek me. I revealed myself to those who made no inquiry about me."[2]

The degree of spiritual maturity that corresponds to the passage from childhood to adolescence is the realization that Jesus is truly God and the full acceptance of that fact by seeking Him by faith, without leaning on natural props and sensible consolations of one kind or another.

Martha went to see Him, that is to say, she went in search of His sensible presence; but Mary stayed home. Why? Because she possessed Him already by faith. When she was sent for, then she was all ready to go. Her admirable discretion is worth observing, especially in the light of what follows. She went to meet Our Lord at His call. She humbled herself before doing anything else. When she showed Him her tears, Our Lord completely melted and gave her more than she dared to ask for.

If seeking Our Lord's sensible presence can be a hindrance, how much more so the seeking of sensible consolations as such, apart from Our Lord. This is the reason for the asceticism of monastic life. Monastic life puts us in a situation where we have to grow up spiritually more quickly than almost any other. As a matter of fact it is precisely by cutting back on the life of the senses and the things that nourish it, that this crisis of faith is precipitated. Spiritual writers like St. John of the Cross have observed that when people begin to lead an ascetical form of life, they quite quickly enter into this crisis of faith. People in ordinary life situations seem to enter it less promptly. This may be because they suffer constant bombardment from distractions of all kinds, which dissipate the time and energy they need to face God and themselves.

But put them in a milieu where sensible consolations are reduced, or teach them not to seek them too ardently, and gradually this crisis begins to come upon them. First of all Our Lord becomes a greater reality in their lives as a human Friend. Then gradually He begins to withdraw and the reality of what living by faith means really strikes home. Our Lord puts to them the question that He so often put to His disciples, whom He was trying to lead into this same crisis: "What's the matter with your faith?[3] ...Why are you fearful, O you of little faith?"[4]

In the Gospel He complains of lack of faith over and over again.[5] Wherever He finds a spark of it, He calls attention to it with admiration and delight[6] —and even with a certain astonishment because it is so rare.

Seek Him for His sensible presence, and He hides. Seek Him by faith, that is, for Himself, and you will find Him. That seems to be the meaning which emerges from the comparison between Martha's prayer and Mary's prayer. Both used exactly the same words, but the same words obtained totally different results.

[1]John 11:20
[2]Rom. 10:20
[3]Luke 8:25
[4]Mark 4:40
[5]Mt. 14:31; 17:20; Luke 9:41; 12:28
[6]Mt. 8:10; 9:29; 15:28, etc.

## IX.  The Goal of the Crisis of Faith

The trials of life, both within and without, are meant by God to mature our souls little by little until we are fully prepared for heaven. That program, however, does not appear as neatly in daily life as it may on paper. Because the very nature of suffering, especially spiritual suffering, is that you suffer, and therefore do not have the consolation of realizing that it is bearing fruit. If you felt you were getting somewhere, it would cease to be suffering; it would be consolation. Once in a while the Lord may lift a corner of the veil and reveal a little fruit that may be ripening. But it is only a corner. The curtains are never drawn completely.

Let us now take a look at other relationships which deteriorate during the crisis of faith.

Someone who enters a monastery, for instance, may well raise this complaint: "Outside everybody treated me nicely, praised me, looked up to me. But here, when I do something wrong, these holy men give me a hard time. They do not seem to appreciate me. They expect me to do jobs I never had before. How can I possibly satisfy them?"

It is a great disappointment to find oneself little appreciated, paid little attention to in a monastery, when outside you had successful friendships and were given credit for being able to accomplish something. If a novice does not realize what is happening, he may find himself asking the question: "Maybe I've come to the wrong place.

I could have done much more good had I remained in the appreciative milieu in which I was a shining light."

Such an attitude, of course, will not get one very far in a monastery, but the feeling of humiliation could be a beginning in the right direction. Our Lord often uses occasions like this to tear down relationships with others which were based on selfish satisfaction. We rendered service to others, we were thanked, we felt pleased with ourselves, and so we had our reward. It is most disappointing to have those gratifications disappear one by one on entering the house of the Lord.

Other interpersonal relationships can become even more demoralizing. St. Teresa, when she went through a trial of this kind, although she had previously been very sociable and pleasant to others, felt a great desire to chew up people. When she got into a little tiff with the other nuns, instead of rising with great ease to *apathia*, as the Greek fathers recommend, she felt the greatest difficulty to keep from sinking her teeth into them. Truly you may ask yourself in this state: "What is happening to me? I never felt this way outside. I wouldn't even swat a fly. But now I feel a strong inclination to take a beam out of the ceiling and crack it down on someone's head."

It is not just the strain of the devout life. It really is the divine action tearing down something. Now the thing God is tearing down is not your virtues, precisely, but your dependence on them, that is, on your own efforts as the means of going to Him. Your own efforts can take you only so far, then gradually their inadequacy shows up. You must be reduced step by step to the situation in which the Canaanite woman found herself when, despairing of all her own resources and with a desperation tempered only by hope in the Lord, she cried out from the bottom of her heart: "Help me!" Two little words which can express grades of meaning which are almost infinite, from the superficial lip service of somebody who has read that he should depend on God, to somebody who has experienced the complete destruction and loss of all his own human resources and who turns to God utterly. The latter is the purpose and goal of the crisis of faith. And it is at that moment that you will get results from the Lord.

In the Gospel of John, just before Our Lord's passion, a group of interested Greek proselytes wanted to see Jesus.[1] Normally Jesus was very gracious about meeting people. For instance, Nicodemus,[2] the Samaritan woman,[3] in fact almost all the people who wanted to meet Him.

But here are these people who said, "We would like to see Jesus." The disciples brought their request to Him and He seems to have paid no attention to it. He was on the very verge of His passion, the purpose for which He had come into the world.

His only reply was, "The hour has come at last for the Son of Man to be glorified. I tell you the plain truth, unless the grain of wheat fall into the ground and die, it remains just one grain. But once it has died, it bears abundant fruit. He who holds his life dear, destroys it, but he who sets no store by his life in this world will preserve it for eternal life."[4]

This was an opportunity for a little apostolic work, to enter into an ecumenical discussion. But at this moment His passion was too close. And no one knew better than Our Lord that it is not through talking, but through His passion and death that people are saved. And so rather than talk to them, He was interested in bringing home to the disciples the importance of submitting to this law of death out of which springs the fullness of life. He wanted to teach them that this growth in our own person is so important, this growth obtained by means of surrendering to the disappointments and sufferings which the divine action sends to us, that compared with it, all other activities—including apostolic activity—should wait until His job has been accomplished, or at least has gotten well under way.

What good, Our Lord seems to say, do you think you can do all by yourself, until you have allowed your natural life to fall into the ground and die so that it can bear fruit?

It is a mistake to imagine, through a misreading of primitive monastic literature, that those who enter upon this way are going to attain to a kind of paradise on earth, spiritual to be sure, but still paradise, filled with ineffable consolations and the uninterrupted enjoyment of their virtues.

The literature on the contemplative life of all ages does in fact hold out the promise of some substantial breakthrough after one has been banged around long enough. One will enter into a wonderful interior freedom where God is within reach at every moment. The experiences of many mystics do in fact lead one to believe that this really happened to them. But we have to understand in what sense this is so. Otherwise we may conclude naively that, if only we stick it out, we will turn into a kind of superman towards the last five or ten years of our life. Then nothing will be able to hurt us anymore.

But the longer you live, the more you realize that these wonderful experiences of the mystics only lasted a short time and that in between they were very much like ourselves. Perhaps the first time we read St. Teresa of Avila we do not pay much attention to the fact that her ecstacies lasted only half an hour. We get the idea they must have lasted half her lifetime. There is a great difference between one half hour and the other twenty-three and a half that have to be lived in an ordinary day.

Any true contemplative life is always going to involve a large proportion of suffering. If for a few moments, even a half hour (or a few days) some great graces come our way, they will make the other twenty-three and a half more burdensome. The great monastic fathers never held out a panacea for our spiritual ills in this life. The Christian life, they said, is perfect only in heaven. Anybody who does not look forward to heaven as his reward is not only going to be disappointed, but is on the wrong road.

How does Our Lord react in this incident recounted by John, in which He seems to experience a kind of foretaste of His passion? He confesses: "Now is my soul shaken in its inmost depths!"[5]

Jesus is nearing the end of His life. He has only a few days to live. And He is terrified at the prospect of dying! He is miserable in an almost infinite degree. There is no question of His passing through a beautiful, peaceful, and painless death into the arms of His heavenly Father. There is a strong cry! There is agony, terrible physical suffering, the sense of abandonment by His Father. The triumph of Jesus is the *acceptance* of that situation, not the enjoyment of it. "Father, save me from this ordeal!" That is Our Lord's reaction to suffering.

But then immediately comes His heroic submission. "No, for this very purpose I have come into the world." In other words, "I want to face the ordeal." But He does not say that it is anything else but an ordeal.

The idea of suffering becoming pure joy or stopping altogether is nonsense. To be a Christian, the Gospel nowhere says that you must relish and savor all the anguish and suffering that can come upon you. Growing up in grace does not mean becoming inhuman or insensible. Our Lord suffered as a man. But there is this difference between Him and us: He was prepared, out of love of His Father, to suffer anything that the Father wanted Him to suffer.

This is what the Canaanite woman did in the face of her outward humiliation and sufferings. She hung on, she trusted, she hoped against hope. These are the dispositions which are truly Christian and which indicate a high degree of spiritual maturity. When the theological virtues of faith, hope, and charity are the principal means by which we go to God, and we are willing to let all other means be taken away—or torn away—when God asks for them, then we are truly imitating Christ; we are His servants.

Jesus in this same incident extends this promise to His servants: "Whoever remains in my personal service (in imitation of my crucifixion) will be honored by my Father."[6]

Not, perhaps, in this life, but certainly in the next one.

[1] John 12:20-36
[2] John 3:1-21
[3] John 4:1-42
[4] John 12:23-26
[5] John 12:27
[6] John 12:26

## X. The Grace of Mary Magdalen

The feast of St. Mary Magdalen is for liturgists a rather perplexing feast. From the time of St. Gregory the Great, if not before, Mary Magdalen has been identified in everybody's mind with the great sinner who washed the feet of Our Lord with her tears and dried them with her hair.[1] Modern research has spoiled everything and discovered that there are really three people who are commemorated in this feast. The feast is named in honor of St. Mary Magdalen. The liturgy recounts her exploits.[2] The Gospel tells about the penitent woman in a town of Galilee, and Mary of Bethany is clearly identified in the prayer of the Mass as the one whose prayers raised Lazarus from the dead. To all appearances then, the liturgy seems to be confused, to say the least.

Actually, on closer examination, the liturgy is not so far wrong after all. Although numerically three distinct feasts would seem to be in order, the Church is really celebrating one great idea, one great spiritual experience. When you compare what happened to these three women, there is something which makes Mary Magdalen one with the penitent woman after she passed through her trial of faith, and one with Mary of Bethany after Jesus raised Lazarus from the tomb. What the Church is celebrating is that sublime degree of confidence and love which results from holding fast to faith in the midst of great trials. These are three women who successfully passed through what I have been calling the crisis of faith. We honor in the liturgy not

only these three women, but everyone who has successfully passed to the love of God through suffering and
humiliation.

Let us compare the experiences of the three women to
see what I mean. Mary of Bethany in her great trial held
fast to faith in the midst of the colossal challenge that Our
Lord threw out to her and Martha, namely, His promise to
raise from the dead the corpse of their brother Lazarus,
already beginning to decompose. She believed without
faltering.

When at Jesus' bidding, Lazarus came forth from the
tomb, what do you suppose her feelings were towards
Jesus? Anyone who has been through any great trial and
who has experienced the divine help in one way or another
will understand what a flood of gratitude poured into her
heart when she realized that her faith in Him had not been
misplaced.

We are not surprised, then, to learn about the lavish
proof of love which Mary of Bethany gave Our Lord at the
supper in Simon the Leper's house six days before the Pass-
over.[3] During the supper she appeared carrying a whole
pound of expensive perfume. Wishing to give expression to
the extent of her love, gratitude, and utter dedication, she
poured out the whole contents of the jar over His head and
feet. This gesture was the symbol, as far as she was concerned, of her whole being. That is why it meant so much
to Jesus. He recognized very clearly what the perfume, together with that lavish gesture, signified, and praised her
extravagance in the face of the outraged economists who
were reclining at table.

Let us look now at Mary Magdalen at the tomb of Jesus.
She had lost Him and was searching for Him with great
heaviness of heart and distraction of mind. He appeared to

her first before anyone else, as a reward for her ardent and eager longing. When He called her by her name, He unloosed in her heart a flood of gratitude and joy. She became completely His possession.

The penitent woman described in Luke was given a similar grace.[4] Her trouble was personal. Mary of Bethany was filled with gratitude to Our Lord for having delivered her brother, whom she loved so much. She is an example of one who reaches this degree of gratitude through love for someone else. She prayed for Lazarus, the symbol of a great sinner, and receiving the extraordinary answer to her prayers, achieved the same inner transformation as that of the penitent woman. In the latter's case it was the forgiveness of her own sins that transformed her into an ocean of love.

We are told that Jesus was invited to the home of a certain Pharisee and reclined at table. Without warning, a woman who was a scandal in the town, came in.

"After making sure that He was at table at the home of the Pharisee, she brought with her an alabaster box of perfume." They must have manufactured alabaster flasks in those days because Mary of Bethany had the same kind of bottle when she anointed Our Lord later on. There are many things which are strikingly similar in the accounts of the two women. However, their temperaments seem to have been quite different.

"She took her stand behind Him at His feet and wept." She certainly was sorry for her sins. She wanted to be forgiven, and she did not know whether she would be. That was her trial. She was not interested in somebody else's sins, but her own. She evidently had plenty.

"Yielding to an impulse," (and it certainly came from the Holy Spirit, judging by the results) "she rained her tears on

His feet and wiped them with her hair. She tenderly kissed His feet and anointed them with perfume."

The embarrassed host noticed all this and said to himself, "This man, if He were a prophet" (that is to say, if He had any discernment) "would know who, and what sort of a creature this woman is who makes such a fuss over Him. She is obviously a scandalous person."

I dare say that it would not have taken much of a prophet to have recognized that she was the lady that she had been. But what she had been, she was no longer, because she was sorry.

Jesus read his thoughts and said, "Simon, I have something to tell you."

"Tell it, Rabbi," he replied.

"Once upon a time, two men were in the debt of a money lender. The one owed him five hundred denarii, the other fifty. Neither of them was in a position to pay, so he made both of them happy by cancelling their debts. Under these circumstances, which of them will be more generous in loving him?"

"The one, I suppose," said Simon, "whom he made happy by cancelling the greater amount."

"Your judgment is correct," Our Lord replied. Then turning to the woman, He said to Simon, "You see this woman? I came into your house. You offered me no water for my feet (the ordinary courtesy). This woman has rained her tears upon my feet and wiped them dry with her hair. You gave me no kiss of welcome (the ordinary courtesy), from the time she entered this woman has not left off tenderly kissing my feet. You did not anoint my head with oil (the ordinary courtesy), this woman has anointed my feet with perfume." Thus Our Lord compares the total lack of the ordinary courtesies which He received from the

Pharisee with the extraordinary marks of courtesy He received from this woman.

What He is really comparing is her response to her forgiveness with the Pharisee's response to his forgiveness, and the conclusion is: "In consideration of this, I tell you, her sins, numerous as they are, are forgiven. You see, she has shown so much love."

And then comes the remark loaded with very heavy irony, "One, of course, who has but little forgiven him, shows but little love."

In other words, "Since you do not think that you are much of a sinner, you cannot be forgiven very much."

This Pharisee is a perfect example of someone who has little self-knowledge, who does not know his own sinfulness, who is more or less well pleased with his virtues and with his service of God, and who is inclined to think that God owes him something. The result of that disposition is an incapacity to give oneself, an incapacity to love.

In this poor penitent woman, we have an example of someone who does know her own misery and wretchedness and how sunk in sin she is, who makes no secret of the fact to herself and to God (and to everybody else for that matter), and who appeals to the love of Christ to save her.

She does not say, "Well, I owe you five hundred denarii and I'll pay you back at the rate of five denarii a month on the installment plan." Oh no! She just collapses at His feet and relies a hundred percent on His mercy.

Imagine what she must have felt when Our Lord turned to her and said, "Your sins are forgiven." That is all she wanted to hear. She did not ask to be a saint, she did not ask to be a mystic, she did not ask to be anything. All she wanted, and wanted desperately, was to get rid of her sins. She contacted Christ on His weak side, because that is precisely the reason that He came down from heaven: "I have come to save that which was lost." Not partially lost, not just what is in bad shape, but what is absolutely hopeless—*shot!*

In other words, He is prepared to build the new creation of grace on *nothing*, which is the way He made the old one. He does not ask for anything except the sincere acknowledgment of need, and hope in His mercy.

She was thrilled when she heard His words. Since the words of the Lord accomplish what they signify, she was instantly forgiven.

The others started grumbling. Who cares what they thought? And she cared a lot less.

Jesus then said to her, "Your faith has saved you."

Faith in what? *Faith in His love.* That is what saved her. She aimed her arrow straight and she hit Our Lord squarely on target, in the center of His heart. She opened for herself and for everybody else who understands her, and who wants to follow in her footsteps, a flood of mercy. Jesus sanctified her at that moment.

Thus the three women commemorated on the feast of St. Mary Magdalen are spiritually one. Each of the persons named in these three instances was reduced, after the manner of the Canaanite woman, to a slender thread of hope. But they hung on, when every human help had been taken away, to faith in His love.

We celebrate in their feast the moment of reward when faith and hope have achieved their work. This is the feast of those who have passed through humiliation and suffering to abiding union with Christ.

[1]Luke 7:36-50      [3]John 12:1-8
[2]John 20:1-18      [4]Luke 7:36-50

## XI. The Sources of Praise

Reflecting on the liturgical feast of St. Mary Magdalen I suggested that although three people were commemorated, they nevertheless are all one spiritually. They came to the deep knowledge of Christ, not by an intellectual penetration, but through the experience of love—the only way that anybody can really come to the knowledge of divine things. They went through trials of faith and hope, and reached God through humiliation and suffering.

Now in the Psalms you have examples of what persons like these say to God after He has given them this grace. Psalm 34 is the song of such a person. It was written by David after he had escaped from the presence of Achish, the Philistine king of Geth.[1]

Here is the background. David was being pursued by Saul. Just before this incident Saul had tried to pin David to the wall with a spear, but missed.[2] Then Saul started tracking him down like a dog in the wilderness.

David escaped to the camp of the Philistine king. Doeg, a man in the hire of Saul, unfortunately was there. Realizing that he was trapped, David hit upon the expedient of acting like a lunatic. That was no small humiliation for the mighty warrior who had slain Goliath, but God wanted to humble him. David began to lean against the wall and to drool on his beard like a madman, making an utter fool of himself.

King Achish, who had been expecting to get a mighty warrior to add to his troops, said, "Why did you bring this lunatic into my presence? Are there not enough fools around here already? Get him out!"

Thus David made good his escape. His response to God's answer to his prayer for deliverance is exactly the same as that of the three women. It is a wonderful response to the gifts of God and to His grace—the only one He asks for. David's heart melted in gratitude to God. You get echoes of this profound disposition of gratitude over and over again in the Psalms. That is why they are such a good teacher of prayer. They teach us what our reaction should be to the gifts of God, and if the spirit of the Psalms ever gets into our bones, we will really know how to pray.

This is exactly the deep spirit of loving gratitude that Mary of Bethany felt when she saw Lazarus coming forth from the tomb after four days of decomposition. Or when the penitent woman realized in the depths of her heart that what she had wanted most, the forgiveness of her sins, had been freely granted by her Savior. They just had to thank Him. The rising tide of loving praise is the inspiration of Psalm 34.

Listen to a few verses of it: "I will bless the Lord at all times. His praise shall ever be in my mouth."

Praise is the fruit of love. The heart of the Church is on fire to praise God. She feels an urgent necessity to thank Him, not just once in a while, but all the time, because of the graces He pours out on the world at every moment. The three women commemorated in the feast of St. Mary Magdalen, and David, are all under the influence of the same grace. They are entering deeper into the heart of the Church, the mystical body of Christ, and they have to praise God. It is a need of love and of gratitude.

He goes on, "Let my soul glory in the Lord; the lowly will hear me and be glad." The lowly, that is to say, those

who have been humbled like me. They will understand
what I am shouting about and why I am jumping up and
down in thanksgiving and joy. God is so good. He has
been so good to me.

"How about glorifying the Lord with me? Let us together extol his name. " His name is what God stands for,
that is, mercy and goodness, which David has just penetrated by experience.

Then he describes what happened: "I sought the Lord
and He answered me, and delivered me from all my fears."
David on this occasion was scared. Like the penitent
woman, he did not know whether the Lord was going to
answer him.

"Look to Him that you may be radiant with joy; and
your faces may not blush with shame." Here is an afflicted
man who called out; and the Lord heard him and from all
his distresses He saved him. "The angel of the Lord en-
camps around those who fear Him, and delivers them."
There is no question in David's mind now about the
continual and sure protection he is going to receive from
the living God.

Here is the line I am most interested in emphasizing:
"Taste and see how good the Lord is; happy the man who
takes refuge in Him."

The Church singles out this verse for several communion
songs. It suggests the mystery of love, the fact that we
know God and attain to a deep knowledge of Him through
love rather than by intellectual reflection.

In the ordinary run of things, we first understand, we
first know, and then we love. For instance, you first study
philosophy or a science for many years, and then you
enjoy seeing problems intuitively solved. But in the supernatural order, it is the reverse. According to the psalmist,

we must first taste, enjoy, and then understand. We must first experience God by love before we can understand Him and respond in the way that David and these women did.

The spiritual senses are an analogy of the material ones: sight, hearing, smell, touch and taste. In bodily things, taste and touch are the most intimate because an object is present directly when you taste or touch it. It is less directly present when you see it, hear it, or smell it. Touch is experienced when an object is immediately present outwardly; taste when an object is present inwardly. God is substantially present in the inmost depths of our souls, and if He makes His presence felt there, the most appropriate analogy of it is taste—the most intimate, the most direct of the experiences of the senses. It is an analogy; not a sensible reality, but a spiritual experience.

The Fathers of the Church remind us over and over again that the experience of the spiritual senses is not possible without the control of our lower nature in such a way that we no longer depend on outward things and natural knowledge to go to God. Purification of the natural senses is required to experience the reality of the spiritual senses. And so David is telling us, inviting us, urging us, to humble ourselves, to take the path that he took, of suffering and humiliation, in order that we may "taste" the highest experience of God and understand how wonderful He is.

*Quoniam suavis est Dominus* is the Latin for "How good the Lord is." That is, how suitable, how well-fitting, how just right, how much like coming home, the experience of the Lord is.

The same word is also used in this saying of Jesus, "Take my yoke upon you because my yoke is easy (*suave*) and my burden light."[3] *Suave* is hard to translate. The idea is that God's will is tailor-made; it suits you, fits every wrinkle of your back.

The experience of God, then, is just right; it fits you to a "t." It is the thing that you have been waiting for. While nothing will be fully satisfying until you get to heaven, still, through the spiritual senses, this experience strikes you as being the answer to all problems—the perfect coming home; something which always should have been there and which you suddenly realize is there. "Taste and see."

The result of this experience is that total turning to God that these three women bear witness to: Mary of Bethany, by emptying the whole bottle of perfume on the head of Jesus;[4] Mary Magdalen, by throwing herself into His arms.[5] We are not told just what the penitent woman did. It is left to our own judgment. But they all could sing in their own way Psalm 34.

If we get through some of our trials, we will sing the same song.

[1] I Samuel 21:11-16
[2] I Samuel 19:8-10
[3] Mt. 11:29-30
[4] Mt. 26:7
[5] John 20:16

## XII. The Greater Grace of John

We have now seen various people in the Gospel success-fully passing through their crisis of faith. I could mention others who did not, but let us stick to those who did. Here are people who have left behind their spiritual diapers, so to speak, and have advanced to adolescence. Now there is nothing wrong with wearing the appropriate garment of one's spiritual age. We all have a very humble beginning as regards our natural life. It would be unreasonable to expect us to have a glorious beginning as regards our supernatural life. We must adapt ourselves to this lowly beginning.

We are still very much beginners if we respond to the events of life in a self-centered way, giving in to the hundred and one emotions and combinations thereof that arise in our hearts from morning to night: those feelings of animosity, discord, anger, hatred, jealousy, envy, impatience, timidity, discouragement, lust. In other words, if pride, ambition, and sensuality dominate our conduct.

While there is nothing wrong with being a beginner, because what else can you do but begin somewhere, still we might well ask ourselves: "How long, O Lord, how long?"[1] At this spiritual age we need a mother, and our Blessed Mother, while she is necessary at every stage, is indispensable here. We need someone to carry us, console us, teach us to walk, pick us up when we fall down, and dry our tears.

The response of faith to the events of life is the sign of

spiritual adolescence. We stop trying to solve our emotional problems by means of selfish motives and try to solve them after the manner of the people we have been observing in the Gospel. Victory is never a hundred percent, but a more or less affair with innumerable regressions.

In the crisis of faith, God asks of us two sacrifices. One is the sacrifice of the desert, and the other is the sacrifice of praise. We saw both of these at work in the incidents already described. The sacrifice of the desert is the sacrifice of bearing with temptation. When we experience the rebellion of our lower nature, we offer ourselves to God in the state of weakness, misery, and apparent defeat. It is the sacrifice of serving God without relish, without feeling that we are getting anywhere—of just plain offering up the daily round of ever recurring duties and ever recurring faults.

But there is also the sacrifice of praise exemplified by the three women commemorated on the feast of St. Mary Madgalen, and in David's hymn, Psalm 34. From time to time in this desert we come to an oasis, and for a few moments God allows us to experience His love and to be conscious of His divine help. When we are up against it and have no strength of ourselves, and cast all our hope on Him; or when we expect to fail but for some extraordinary reason, which can only be the grace of God, do not; then there wells up a flood of gratitude, very gentle at times, at other times like a tidal wave. Call it consolation if you wish. At least it is the consolation of not having failed, of not having surrendered to temptation and sin.

Our Lord Himself experienced the sacrifice of the desert. It was, in fact, in the desert that He suffered temptation. He also allowed Himself to feel the terrible undertow of human weakness. It caused Him to cry out in His agony to be spared His passion and death, the very redemptive act which He was looking forward to so eagerly throughout His life. We also look forward in moments of fervor to serving God greatly, and then when the moment arrives and the Lord offers us the sacrifice of the desert, we suddenly face a cross that looks to be completely beyond our strength. Our knees begin to knock together, and we say to the Lord, "Please, could we postpone this for a few days—just until I feel a little more spiritual strength?"

He says, "Not tomorrow, but today." If we get through it, there follows that deepening of trust which comes from experiencing God's help when we did not really expect it, and yet hoped against hope.

Both of these sacrifices are frequent in the growing up process. Indeed we have need of both. We need to experience our weakness and we need to experience the divine strength over and over again before we can attain the age of spiritual adolescence.

There is a very special grace which is connected with the sacrifice of praise. It should be distinguished from that of Mary of Bethany when she was at Our Lord's feet and absorbed more in Himself than in His words. She clearly was growing up interiorly. She was receiving from Him a deeper understanding of the mysteries that He was teaching her.

But there is a still greater grace described in the Gospel of John.[2] Our Lord had just washed the feet of the disciples. It was a magnificent example of humility, and must have evoked great admiration in the heart of John. It undoubtedly awakened in him a new depth of love for Our Lord.

"When Jesus had said this, He was shaken in His inmost

soul and with great emphasis He declared, 'I tell you truly, one of your group is about to betray me!' "

Once again we see Him suffering with suffering and not with joy. It was the sacrifice of the desert which Our Lord allowed Himself to feel, the agony which every human heart feels when betrayed by someone whom it loves.

"The disciples then looked at one another, at a loss to know whom He meant. Now one of the disciples of Jesus lay resting in His bosom, the one whom Jesus loved." *Bosom* means the hollow of the breast. Thus John had his ear tucked up against the heart of Christ. He was close enough to hear it pounding in response to the knowledge of its betrayer.

We might well ask, "How did John get there?" The ancients, when they went to supper, leaned on their left elbow. Thus it would not be too difficult for him, because he was so close, to snuggle up and to lay his head against the breast of Jesus.

Now Peter had something he wanted to say to Our Lord. He saw that John was in a position to speak to Him without anyone else hearing, so he whispered, "Ask whom He means."

"Then he, freely drawing close to Jesus' breast, said to Him, 'Who is it, Master?' "

We already saw him resting in the hollow of Jesus' breast. How could he get any closer? Perhaps he drew away for a moment to listen to Peter. In any case, the position of John is most significant. We saw the penitent woman washing His feet; we saw Mary of Bethany pouring perfume over His head; but we are in the presence here of a greater grace. What does the bosom of Jesus represent? And what does it mean to rest your head in His bosom?

First of all, we know that Abraham's bosom was a symbol for the Jews of perfect happiness, intimacy, protection, security, familiarity. Intimacy, then, is certainly one of the notes. We read in the parable of the rich man and Lazarus[3] how the poor man, Lazarus, was carried to Abraham's bosom, where he was having a grand time. That is the place where everyone wanted to go. If Abraham's bosom is paradise, what about the bosom of Jesus?

John speaks elsewhere of the only begotten Son, "who is in the bosom of the Father." It would seem then that John, resting in Our Lord's bosom, was being carried by Him into the bosom of the Father.

Paul says, "Christ is the head of every man...and God is the head of Christ."[4] As John rested in Jesus' bosom, Christ was becoming completely his head.

The disciples at this moment were about to receive the Eucharist. John, characteristically, is a little ahead of the others in spiritual perception. Perhaps Our Lord is trying to teach him what the Eucharist really means: it is not so much a taking of Christ into ourselves, as of His taking us into Himself. Each reception of the Eucharist is an insertion of the branches, which we are, deeper into the Vine, who is Christ. So at this moment, this little branch, John, is being inserted more deeply into the Vine. What he experienced there is not said, but it is evident that the position that he held entitled him to know secrets which the others were not entitled to know.

Our Lord reveals to him three things: first of all, the person who is to betray Him; secondly, the great love that He has for the betrayer; finally, the agony which His heart is suffering at His betrayal.

Jesus' answer is, "It is he to whom I will give the morsel after dipping it in the bowl."

This gesture was traditionally one of friendship. It can be interpreted as a last attempt on Our Lord's part to show His love for His betrayer. He showed him that He knew who he was and yet still was offering His friendship.

"So He dipped the morsel and with His own hand reached it to Judas. Directly after the morsel Satan entered into him and he went out, and it was night."

To rest in the bosom of Jesus is not to be idle. Because, as Jesus tells us, "The Father works until now and I work." This rest is something special; it is not just a nap. It is different from the leisure, however holy, that Mary was enjoying at the feet of Christ. This is rather the grace to rest in God no matter what you are doing. It is a greater grace because it unites action and contemplation. This grace that John had was the grace of Mary and Martha combined; it required a greater spiritual maturity.

It is one thing to be able to pray and to rest in God when everything is quiet and peaceful. It is another to be able to rest in Him when you are running for a commuter train or catching finished goods flying off the end of a machine. It is a greater grace to be able to talk to other people and still be resting in God, than to have to stop talking to anyone in order to speak to God. It is a greater grace than Mary had because it involves greater liberty of spirit, greater intimacy with God. It brings us to the threshold of the crisis of love.

The rest of which John is the symbol consists in the calm of those hundred and one passions. They are in repose because faith has conquered them. Not that we no longer feel them. But the habit of referring everything to God and of flying to Him for refuge, together with the experience of being delivered, has brought us a profound stability of soul. It is the Sabbath rest, of which Sunday is the symbol, and of which heaven is the perfect fulfillment.

"Eternal rest grant unto them, O Lord," is the prayer the Church offers for those who sleep in the Lord. That does not just mean sitting down under a heavenly palm tree. It means the fruition of all our desires in the possession of the object for which they were intended, the Triune God.

The rest of which John is a symbol in this scene is the rest which comes to those who are most active in love, the highest form of activity open to man in this life. The fullness of love brings the maximum of rest at the same time that it makes possible the maximum of action.

Our Blessed Mother is the exemplar of this grace. That is why, on the feast of the Assumption in the Cistercian liturgy, the Gospel of Mary and Martha is read.[5] As the perfect contemplative, she unites in herself the capacity to work for God and to rest in God, which belongs to those who have passed through the crisis of faith and of love, and who have entered interiorly into the Sabbath of the Lord

[1]Ps. 74:9-10
[2]John 13:1-30
[3]Luke 16:19-31
[4]I Cor. 11:3
[5]Luke 10:38-42

## XIII. The Absence of Jesus

We have seen a number of people in the Gospel, all of whom might be characterized as wanting something: the royal official, the centurion, Mary of Bethany, Martha of the same place, Mary Magdalen, the Canaanite woman and the penitent woman. These people all asked Our Lord for something. They endured suffering and humiliation, but it was in order to obtain some favor in contradistinction to those many persons whose prayers He just answered. Our Lord took these in hand, so to speak, leading them step by step from a weak faith to a strong, living faith—a faith which He gradually transformed into hope. The result of their hope in Him was a complete turning to God, a conversion in the full sense of the word. This is the final resolution of the crisis of faith.

The original message of the Gospel, remember, is: "Do penance, for the kingdom of God is accessible, nearby."[1]

"Do penance" means "be converted," or "have a change of heart." It does not mean "do this series of religious exercises, endure this series of trials, find yourself this degree of austerity;" but "allow your inmost heart to be changed."

This is exactly the fruit of the crisis of faith. It changes radically, inwardly, *most inwardly*, your values, your faith, your hope, and your love. Mary of Bethany turned to Our Lord from the depths of her being after she saw her brother come forth from the tomb. She achieved in that moment the total dedication of herself to God. She expressed it by the lavish gesture of pouring out the perfume of her love over Him at the supper in Simon the Leper's house.

We identified the crisis of faith as the first part of the growing up process. There is a further crisis which should be pointed out in order to understand fully "the breadth and length and the height and depth"[2] of the love of God, to which we are invited through the grace of Baptism. It corresponds to the passage from adolescence to adulthood.

The second crisis is a purification of love.

Do we need a purification of love?

Recall the incidents of Mary of Bethany, the Canaanite woman, and the penitent woman when she received the assurance of the forgiveness of her sins. The wave of gratitude pouring into their hearts, causing them to overflow with love and praise, must have been something that did not wear off in a few hours or a few days. It established each of them in a stable union with Our Lord. Practically speaking, they hoped in His mercy, a hope which henceforth made them strong despite discouragement, trials, difficulties, and even the death of the Lord Himself.

Let us suppose then, that we, by the grace of God, have had our faith purified and have experienced our hope and trust ripening into love. We know we love Our Lord and are seeking not so much His favors, but Himself. Would you think that such a strong love still needed purification?

Let us take a look at our Blessed Mother.[3] One might think that she, at least, was perfect in love and grace from the beginning. But God's idea of love is different from ours.

The Holy Family went dutifully every year to the temple at Jerusalem according to the Jewish custom. On one occasion when Jesus was twelve years old, He disappeared. Mary and Joseph had started home and had gone a day's journey before they missed Him. They retraced their steps to Jerusalem to seek Him. They searched for three days. It was a preview of His death for Our Lady, and for Joseph, his last great trial. After that we hear no more of him.

We are tempted to ask the same question that she did when she finally found her Son. Why could not Jesus have told her what He was going to do? Nowadays if a boy runs away from home, he is considered a disturbed child and is liable to wind up in the hands of a social worker.

They searched far and wide for Him. When loving parents have lost a child, each one's sorrow increases that of the other. They must have been distraught after three sleepless days and nights. Their astonishment can well be imagined when they found Him in the temple, in the midst of the rabbis, apparently having a very good time. Whether He had been arguing all that time, the Gospel does not say. Everyone was charmed with His intelligence and His answers.

His parents were overjoyed to see Him and embraced Him. Our Blessed Mother could not resist just a word of reproof in spite of her joy. After all, He was her child. She said to Him the ordinary thing any mother would say to her boy who has run away from home or disappeared without saying anything: "Son, why did you do this to us? Oh, our hearts were heavy, your father's and mine, as we searched for you!"

Even our Blessed Mother could not hide her feelings at this moment. Her sorrow had been so great. Just speaking of it eased the tension. But He showed no sign of apologizing, and gave every evidence of being quite satisfied with the situation.

Then comes an extraordinary statement. Only God could administer such a rebuke! Here is a broken-hearted mother, His own mother, and Joseph, trying to hide his own feelings. Jesus says, "Why did you look for me? Didn't you know"—in other words, you should have known—"that I had to be about my Father's business?"

"But they did not grasp the meaning of the reply He made to them." They were stunned.

Having said this, having made it perfectly clear where He stood and where they stood, "He went down to Nazareth and was subject to them." That was His Father's business for the moment—and indeed for many years.

Our Blessed Mother must be the one who related this incident to Luke. Who else could have told him? She wanted us to know that she, too, had to be reminded that God's will has to come before every other duty and affection, including the most legitimate, including those willed by Him, such as the love of a son for his mother.

Our Blessed Mother had no original sin. All her feelings and emotions were submissive to her will. She was a perfect child of grace. But even she needed to be reminded by Our Lord of the primacy of the Father's will. Although she was perfectly united to that will during the trial of searching for her Son, she was confused by His conduct towards her. As in all the cases of His enigmatic answers or seeming rebukes, the reply of Jesus was an invitation to a new abyss of purity of heart, to a new expansion of divine love. He reminds His Mother: "Don't forget, I'm not just your little boy. I am the Son of the living God. He is my Father. I must be doing the work my Father has entrusted to me."

Notice the implication that Joseph is not His father in the ordinary sense.

Jesus had always been a dutiful son up to this point. Did they need to be reminded that He belonged not so much to them as to the Father, and that the Father's will must come before everything else, including *them?*

Of course, how could they know—He was only twelve—that the will of the Father was going to require this special mission of His Son and leave them out in the cold?

This same sort of situation is going to happen to us also just when we think we are loving Our Lord to the best of our ability and are experiencing His love for us. Just when things are calm and quiet, and when we have successfully passed through trials of faith and reached what feels like an unconquerable hope in the Lord, all of a sudden, for no apparent reason, comes a new call to purify our hearts and open them up again to the inner searchings of divine love.

When this Gospel is proclaimed in the liturgy of the Christmas season, the prayer of the day asks that we be shown, "the good, the acceptable, and the perfect will of God." This prayer suggests that there are three degrees of submission to the will of God. The good will of God is His will above every sin. The acceptable will of God is His will above every other affection. And the perfect will of God is His will above every other love including ourselves.

In our Blessed Mother there was never any doubt about her submission to God's will from every point of view. Yet He willed to go on perfecting the purity of her adherence to the will of His Father.

Having reminded her, He packed His bags and went down with her to Nazareth and became once again a very dutiful son—until the moment He had to leave her permanently, in order to bring to completion the redemption of the world.

[1]Mt. 4:17                    [2]Eph. 3:18                    [3]Luke 2:41-52

## XIV.  The Patience of Job

Jesus upset the sublime tranquillity of the most beautiful home-life any couple ever enjoyed, by reminding them of His unique character. He seems to have tried to purify their motivation. If their intention needed purification, what of ours?

Let us look at a similar situation in the Old Testament story of Job.[1] Whether he is a legendary character or a real man is beside the point; the message remains the same. It may be disappointing to realize that some of our great friends in the Old Testament may be only legends, but if that is the truth, we have to accept it. In any case, all that Job represents, and all the Jobs down through the centuries, really have existed.

He represents a person who has attained a profound and stable union with God. He is described as a very rich man. His great possessions, symbols of his interior state, are enumerated. His many works of virtue, his generous charity, his innocence of life also are enumerated. God Himself acknowledges His great satisfaction with Job's conduct.

His good life began to awaken the jealousy of Satan. If anyone thinks he can be sanctified without a few tiffs with Satan, he is going against twenty centuries of Christian tradition and experience. You do not have to depart for the desert like St. Anthony of Egypt to challenge him. If you just try to behave yourself, he will show up soon enough.

Job was minding his own business, leading a life of holiness and edifying everybody. From the text you would be led to think that he was almost ready to pass from this life to the life of glory.

However, the text continues: "One day when the heavenly powers stood waiting upon the Lord's presence and among them man's Enemy, the Lord asked him where he had been. 'Roaming about the earth,' said he, 'to and fro about the earth.' 'Why then,' the Lord said, 'you have seen a servant of mine called Job. Here is a true man, an honest man, there's nobody like him on earth. He always fears his God and keeps far from wrong-doing.' "

Satan's reply expresses well his jealousy towards all such people, as well as his insolence. He is not afraid to say to God, "Job fears his God and loses nothing by it. Sheltered his life by your protection, sheltered his home and his property, your blessing is on everything he undertakes. His worldly goods still go on increasing. Why he loses nothing from serving you! One little touch of your hand, however, assailing all that wealth of his, then see how he will turn and blaspheme you."

God had no answer for that. He had to admit the possibility. Job's virtue had in fact not been fully proved. "Okay," the Lord answered, "with all his possessions do what you will as long as you leave himself unharmed." With that the Enemy left the Lord's presence.

We cannot blame God for this situation. The devil exists. You cannot escape Satan's jealousy once you begin growing up in the life of grace. But God uses the devil's own cunning to cause His servants to grow faster and stronger. Job was one of those people in whom the crisis of love was initiated by a series of unexpected personal tragedies, involving his possessions, his family, and finally his own health.

He was sitting down having a glass of wine at the house of his eldest brother. A string of messengers bringing bad news file in. The first announced that his oxen and asses had been taken away and all his men killed except one; the second, that his sheep were destroyed by lightning; the third, that some bandits had driven off all his camels. Just as he was recovering from these blows, a fourth messenger arrived saying that all his sons and daughters were in a house when a tempest arose; the roof caved in, and they were all killed.

What was Job's reaction? "He rose up and rent his garments about him, shaved his head, and fell down to earth to do reverence."

He expresses his unwavering faith and utter resignation in these words: "Naked I came when I left my mother's womb, and whence I came, naked I must go. The Lord gave, the Lord has taken away. Nothing has here befallen but what was the Lord's will. Blessed be the name of the Lord."..."In all this Job guarded his lips well nor challenged with human folly God's wisdom."

That is the end of Chapter One. You would think that he could have received right then the martyr's palm. He has arrived at the same high level of love as the three women commemorated on the feast of St. Mary Magdalen and King David. But now this very love is being put to the test. Job remains united to God's will in the midst of his grief, thus proving that he loves God above all his possessions and more than his family.

Now comes Chapter Two. Satan is not through with him yet by any means. "Once again the heavenly powers came to wait upon the Lord's presence and there, waiting with the rest of them, was the Enemy of man. And of his

travels he still said the same. He had been roaming about
the earth, to and fro about the earth.

" 'Why, then,' said the Lord, 'you have seen for yourself
this servant of mine, Job. There is nobody like him on
earth, a man so true and honest, ever fearing his God and
keeping far from wrongdoing.' "

Thus God, after this set of trials, was able to give him
the same encomium as on the first occasion. And He
added: "Shame it is that you would set me on to do him a
mischief, and all to no purpose."

Evidently God is reluctant with this business of proving
Job. He is sort of forced into it by the miserable ill humor
of the devil.

"No," answered the Enemy, "skin for skin. Nothing a
man owns but he will part with it to keep his skin whole.
That hand of yours, let it fall on bone of his, flesh of his.
Then see if he does not turn and blaspheme you."

In these words the devil urges God to test the purity of
Job's love to see whether he really loves Him above all
things, including himself.

The three women and David were prepared to love God,
but they also were hoping for favors. They all asked for
something. Even those who are trying to serve God very
generously tend to want at least some sign of recognition.
The question raised here is: do we really love God for
Himself alone and for no other reason than because He is
infinitely lovable?

This does not mean we should not value the desire of
getting to heaven. But the desire of heaven can become at
times very remote; so remote, in fact, that it seems to
disappear. God allows it to be buried for a time to enable
His servant to reach that perfect purity of love which can
only come about through profound purification. This sort

of trial is not as rare as you may think. God singles out for special treatment those whom He loves the most, and He will not let up until He has accomplished His end. The tremendous challenge of Christian life is that God is willing to go the whole way in giving Himself to us if we will go the whole way in giving ourselves to Him.

Getting back to Job's story, God was impressed with the arguments of the Enemy and said, "He is in your power provided his life be kept safe."

With that the Enemy left the Lord's presence. He smote Job, an absolutely innocent man. To be exact: "He smote Job with a foul scab from head to foot so that he was feign to sit down on the dunghill and scratch himself with a shard where he itched. Little comfort his own wife gave him.

" 'What,' she said, 'still priding yourself on your innocence? Better you should curse God and die.'

" 'Spoken like a foolish wife,' Job answered. 'What, should we accept the good fortune God sends us and not the ill!' So well even now did Job guard his lips."

How often it happens, when you are down and out, that someone comes along and kicks you in the teeth, or says something to you that could not be more indiscreet. But that is part of this business of being in God's special favor. He concentrates on you.

As for Job, God not only allowed this to happen to him, but He took away all his friends and sent him three "comforters," who plied him with pious platitudes and accused him of all kinds of things that he had never done. It really was these false comforters that eventually became just too much for Job.

"Have pity on me, at least you, my friends," he pleaded

with them. In other words, "Won't you please leave me alone!"

The false comfort they offered is what caused him finally to lose patience. The patience of Job is proverbial, though close scrutiny of the text suggests that it did not hold out much farther than Chapter Two.

"News of the calamity that had befallen him reached three of his friends," and when they showed up, they could scarcely recognize him. "Loud they cried out and sore they wept, tore their garments about them, and heaped the dust high on their heads, and for seven days and seven nights they sat there on the ground beside him and no word spoken. Here, they saw plainly, was overmastering grief."[2]

What could they say to Job? They should have kept quiet.

"At last Job himself broke into utterance and fell to cursing the day on which he was born. 'Blotted out forever be the day of my birth....Had but the womb been the tomb of me! Had I died at birth...all would be rest now, all would be silence. Deeply I would take my repose with the old kings and senators...with the still-born and babe unborn, hidden away in the sunless grave. There the unquietness of the wicked is stilled, and the weary are at rest....Why should they ever see the light that groan to see it? Why should they live, that must live in bitterness of soul? Why should they long for death, like treasure seekers, a grave the prize they covet? Such men as I, that must tread blindfold in the maze of God's making! Ever as I sit down to meat the sighs come. Grief floods over me unrestrained. Must I have nothing left to daunt me? Must each calamity be felt as soon as feared? And still I kept my own counsel, still patient and silent I, till my angry mood overcame me at last.' "[3]

There is a great mystery in the suffering of the innocent. Perhaps it is better just to accept it as a mystery rather than to try to exlain it. Apparently Job did not take Satan into consideration in his complaints. Step by step, materially then spiritually, as you see from the text, especially as we read on, he is left with only one thread of consolation: the fact that God is God, the Creator who can do whatever He likes; and nobody can say to Him, "You can't do that to me."

As he is reduced gradually to the acceptance of that fact, and to silence, the purity of his love grows apace. In the end, God made Job twice as rich (again a symbol of his interior grace) as he was before his trials began.

[1] Job 1 and 2
[2] Job 2:11-13
[3] Job 3:1ff

## XV.  The Widow's Mite

Another light on the crisis of love is given us in Luke's Gospel. If you understand these four verses you have understood Our Lord. It is one of the great revelations of God in Scripture.

Jesus one day was making a visit to the temple when, "Looking up He saw the people putting their offerings into the treasury."[1]

It may have been a box like modern churches have at the door. In any case, He had His eye on how the collection was going. Some well-to-do folk were dropping offerings into the box. He noticed a poor widow put in two small coins. At this His eyes filled with joy and perhaps tears, and He said to His disciples, "I tell you the plain truth. This widow, the beggar woman that she is, has put in more than all the others. For all these other people took from their superfluities what they put in as offerings to God, but this woman, in her extreme want, put in all that she had to live on."

Just before this event, Our Lord had a few words to say about the Scribes. "Beware of the Scribes who fancy fine robes for outdoor wear and crave ceremonious greetings in public places and front seats in the synagogues and places of honor at meals. These men that devour the fortunes of widows ana recite long prayers for show will receive a more than ordinary punishment."[2]

Our Lord despises show in general, especially a pious show. And then comes this sweet little lady. She had no idea that Jesus noticed what she did. As far as we know, she never knew what a hit she made with Our Lord until she got to heaven. He did not call her aside afterwards and pat her on the back. Nor was there any refund for her generous offering.

Who is this widow? First of all, she was a widow, that is to say, she had no husband to support her. She was also a beggar woman. She had lost all material support. She put her money "into the treasury," by which we may understand the treasury of the Church, out of whose merits all sinners are saved and saints are sanctified. She put in all she had, which was two small coins. We might take these two small coins to stand for what constitutes human nature, namely, body and soul. She had no superfluities, that is to say, she had nothing to offer except body and soul. But because it was all she had, she put in more than all the others.

Does not that remind us of the doctrine, repeated over and over again in the Gospel, that what God is looking for from us is a gift, not just out of our pocket money, but out of our inmost being: the gift of self? That gift is more precious than all other things that we can offer Him, which might be called superfluities: natural gifts, such as preaching, teaching, administration, sociability; charismatic gifts, such as the gift of tongues, working miracles, healing the sick. These are the superfluities which many good people are generously dropping into the treasury of the Church.

Along comes this widow. She is a symbol of a life entirely orientated to seeking God and nothing else.

She has very little that shows to offer. She has only her poverty, loneliness, and weakness—her extreme want.

This is exactly the sacrifice that Job, after the devil went to work on him, was offering to God upon the dunghill.[3]

All his good things, his human achievements, his dignities—what I call here his "superfluities"—had been taken away, and he was offering to God the radical gift, the gift of himself.

If you have penetrated the meaning of this incident, you have understood the mystery of a hidden life of prayer and its power. Although we certainly want to make reasonable use of our talents, serve others, and do our duties well, these are not the most essential things. The gift that God wishes us to offer is much more difficult than all other kinds of service because it is the total gift of our being—our inmost self—whatever this actually is. It usually includes much misery, weakness, sinfulness. And this is what tends to predominate in our consciousness. This offering out of our spiritual destitution is a gift for which there may be no refund in this life. We please Our Lord when we have nothing to show for long years of service and yet still go on serving Him. But when such a person gets to heaven, there is going to be a tremendous revelation!

Few people aspire to this gift. Perhaps that is why the Church is in such a bad state today. These two small coins, or rather the total gift of self which they represent, do not fall into the "treasury" too often. Our Lord was looking at the treasury precisely to obtain for Himself the joy of seeing this little widow come along and drop in—they made no noise because they were so small—her tiny gift. That is, after all, what the hidden life means, a gift that is not especially noticeable. Its apostolic power consists in the fact that it moves the Heart of Christ, the source of all grace, so profoundly.

¹Luke 21:1-4                    ²Luke 20:45-47                    ³Job 2:8

## XVI. The Reward of the Widow's Mite

The offering of this widow is substantially the same as that of Mary of Bethany.[1] You remember she offered Our Lord the entire contents of a bottle of perfume. There was nothing surprising about offering perfume. Everybody knew that she loved Our Lord, and that perfume was a good symbol of that love. But what caused the astonishment of everybody present at the supper and the indignation of at least one of the disciples was the lavishness of the gift, the extraordinary gesture of pouring out, not just a few drops of the costly liquid, but *everything that was in the jar.*

"Here it is," she said, speaking by action rather than by words. A little drop was all that was expected...Bang! She *smashed* the whole bottle over His head! No thought of leaving a little aside for tomorrow, or for somebody else, or for herself. No thought of the price. The *lavishness* of the gift, that is the essential point of the story. That is what moved Our Lord so much. That is why He wanted this incident to be recorded for all ages to come, "wherever the Gospel is preached."[2]

Now the sweet little old lady, the Gospel tells us, offered "all that she had to live on."[3] It was numerically not much—two small coins—but it was all she had. Our Lord immediately noticed it and brought it to the disciples' attention in exactly the same way that He publicized the offering of His friend, Mary of Bethany.

It is vanity for us to aim at offering something great in

this world's eyes or in our own. Intellectual people harbor a secret hope of reaching Our Lord by means of their brilliance. Strong willed people hope to reach Him by means of their austerities or activities. Both of these approaches are useful but not ultimate. They are only means. If we are strongly inclined to one or the other, we may tend to make them ends instead of means.

What Our Lord values is the surrender of a truly humble heart. No other means will ever reach Him, not at least in the sense of perfect union. It is so easy and yet so hard. You do not have to have anything special to offer, but it does have to be your all.

In the school I attended as a boy there was a very well-thought out athletic program designed to keep the youngsters busy during their free time. It consisted of a series of athletic contests such as chinning, climbing a rope ladder or a pole, broad jump, high jump, etc. For each of these contests a certain number of points were awarded, and at the end of the year the boy with the highest number of points received a beautiful loving cup with his name inscribed on it.

The athletic director was one of those genial characters often found in charge of athletic programs, affectionately known as "Chief." One of the most difficult and exciting contests was rope climbing. For this event he used to have in hand a very large stop-watch. The contestants would step forward, put their hands on the rope, and when Chief said, "Go!" they would start climbing. If you reached the top in ten seconds, you got ten points; six seconds, sixty points; three seconds, a hundred and fifty points. You had to be pretty wiry and strong to go up that fast. The pole climb provided a little friction for sweaty feet, but for rope climbing these did not help. It had to be all muscle.

Some of the youngsters used to go shooting up the rope with great speed. Now there was one fellow, Joe by name, who was an intellectual. As often happens in the case of intellectuals at that age, he was very fat. Joe found this particular part of the athletic program extremely humiliating. He could not in fact get off the ground.

Everytime the rope-climbing contest came he would go through the motions of grasping the rope. Chief would say, "Go!" Then Joe would dangle helplessly amid the jeers of his companions. It was a good chance for them to get even with him for those straight A's he got in the classroom. The effort would make Joe's neck bulge and his face would turn very red. His companions would call out, "What's the matter, Joe? Hurry up!...Next!"

One day when the rope-climbing contest came around and Joe's name was called out for his turn, he stoutly declined. Chief was a shrewd man and had an eye out to train these boys.

"Joe, aren't you going to make at least a try at climbing the rope?" Chief inquired.

Joe said, "No." There was a lot of hooting from the crowd.

Chief puffed heavily on his cigar and, looking squarely at Joe, challenged him with this offer: "I'll give you one point for trying."

One point for trying! Others that day had been getting sixty, eighty, and a hundred points. It did not sound like much of an offer. But Joe stepped forward, despite the jeers of his companions, put his hands on the rope, and dangled there in his customary helpless position. He huffed and puffed for thirty or forty seconds, got nowhere, and withdrew. It was the usual failure. Meanwhile, Chief, with a great flourish of the pen, put down one point after Joe's name.

Somebody else of course won the loving cup. But whom do you think would have received it if the same Person who noticed the poor widow had been Joe's scorekeeper?

When the recording angels were going over the figures at the end of the school year, they saw that many had received hundreds of points. When they came to Joe's name, they saw only one. But they also saw the humiliation that went into that one point for trying. They took their pencils and started adding zeros. He wound up with millions of points.

From God's point of view, it is not accomplishments but efforts that count. If we accept our poverty and limitations, but still go on trying, we will rate higher than everybody else in Our Lord's book, just as the poor widow did. After all, who made her a beggar woman? It was the divine action, and the same divine action is gradually making us beggars also, pushing us to the extremity which Job symbolizes, where we have nothing left to offer. Yet Jesus still asks us to try to make efforts, even though we know they will not succeed. To obey, to hold back the critical word, to be kind to an enemy, not to dwell on this evil thought or that evil desire, seems at times impossible. God encourages us saying, "I'll give you one point for trying!"

Here is the reason. If we make the effort and receive that one precious point for trying, God can take His pencil and start adding zeros after it. But if that crucial point is missing, no amount of zeros can help. Our score will be just plain "zero."

What did Our Lord mean when He said of the poor widow and her offering, "She put in more than all the others"? She actually put in only two small coins. But He knew that He was adding zeros so that she would turn up with the loving cup. She really got the first prize, but without knowing it. It never entered her mind that she was doing something great. True greatness scarcely recognizes itself. Its left hand does not know what its right hand is doing.[4]

Our Lord's doctrine is wonderful. He goes right to the inmost heart of reality and presents us with true values, cutting across all sham, show, superficiality, the secondary, and the accidental. "My son, give me the gift of your heart."[5] That is what He wants. With that gift He can add everything else. But without it our score with Him will always be very low no matter how much the audience may applaud.

[1]Mt. 26:6-7
[2]Mt. 26:13
[3]Luke 21:4
[4]Mt. 6:3
[5]Prov. 23:26

## XVII.   PETER: The Formation of a Disciple

This account of Peter's preparation for his mission is written for those who are interested in becoming apostles of
Jesus Christ and want to know how to go about it. Much
can be learned from the way Our Lord trained His first
disciples and formed them into apostles. Peter happens to
be the man most clearly characterized in the Gospel. It is
for that reason I will concentrate on him and on the
training which Jesus personally gave him.

1.

Peter was an ordinary guy. He ran a little fishing business on the Sea of Galilee. He lived with his mother-in-
law, a fact which hints at what a fine man he was. His wife
probably had died. We find no mention of her in the
Gospels. Peter was full of natural ardor, impetuosity, had
his share of ambition, liked being a big shot (or at least the
center of attention), had a commanding way of saying and
doing things, enjoyed a certain amount of leadership
ability, and suffered from a whole slue of human failings.
It is not my purpose, of course, to run down Peter. What I
will try to show is that, when Our Lord decides to choose
somebody like us and to make something out of us, it is
*His* idea not ours. *He* is the one who has the most stock in
this business, and *He* is the one who is going to make it
succeed—and that in spite of us!

The Gospels are a mirror in which we can sometimes
see, if we look closely, what God is doing in our own souls
right here and now. In the day-to-day encounters Jesus had

with people coming to Him, and in His developing relationships with His disciples, we recognize examples or symbols of the way we are encountering Him and the way He is relating to us and working in us today. He has not changed much since His Ascension. He has just become more powerful.

Let us take a look at the call of the first disciples. Jesus had led His hidden life for thirty years. No one knew who He was yet, not even John the Baptist. John had been told that he would recognize the Messiah, the Son of God, when he saw a dove descending upon Him. This was the only sign he had been given.

Now John had disciples of his own; in fact Andrew, the brother of Peter, and John, the Beloved Disciple, were his disciples first.

When Our Lord's Baptism took place and John saw the Dove descending upon Him, as had been foretold, he realized that Jesus was the Son of God. He started dropping hints to his own disciples: "The Messiah, the Son of God, the One whom everyone has been waiting for, has come."

One day John was at his usual place along the Jordan together with these two disciples, when Jesus passed by. Fixing his eyes on Jesus and making sure that his two disciples heard him, he said: "Look! There is the Lamb of God!"

When they heard this remark and watched Jesus walking along, they were fascinated by Him. They started following Him, without knowing quite why, along the bank of the river. Of course, Our Lord looked around to see what was going on—nobody likes to be trailed—and said to them, "What would you like?"

They did not know just what to answer. They were embarrassed to be caught trailing Him. "Where do you live?" they stammered for lack of something better to say.

He replied, "Come and see." They followed. He graciously invited them into His tent, and they spent the rest of the day with Him.

John reflected on this experience many years later when writing his Gospel, and recorded the exact time of the encounter: "It was the fourth hour." This moment of his life, when he first came to know Christ, was so stamped on his memory that it could never be forgotten. It was so indelibly engraved there that he could pinpoint the exact moment as long as he lived.

At some moment in our lives, this may happen to us, too. We may be riding in a taxi; we may be dangling our legs over the edge of a swimming pool; we may be reading a book; we may even be in a church—it does not really matter. At some point, if Our Lord is after us—that is the main point—He makes us aware that He wants us to do something for Him—something important. In substance He says, "How about it? Will you be my disciple?"

As soon as Andrew and John met Jesus, they were so enthused that they wanted to tell their friends and relatives all about Him. Andrew told his brother Peter and introduced him to Our Lord at the earliest opportunity.

When Jesus met Peter, He looked at him very intently and said: "You are Simon (that was his ordinary name), son of John, but you are to be called Cephas (which means in our language, Peter)."

"Peter" is a nickname: it means "Rocky." See how human Our Lord was—the first time He met this big, burly fisherman, He said, "Hi, Rocky, how are you?"

Why did Jesus call this man "Rocky"? Maybe it was because he was a big bruiser. Maybe it was because of his stubbornness; or maybe it was his head. Anyway, the nickname seems to have intrigued his friends because it has stuck with him down to the present day. Under the great dome of Saint Peter's basilica in Rome in letters eighteen feet high, you can read the words, "TU ES PETRUS"—"YOU ARE ROCKY."

Some might contend that the nickname was meant to be prophetic of the fact that one day Peter would be the foundation stone of the Church. From the human point of view, however, no one was less like a rock than Peter. He was so unstable, impetuous, and unreliable. No one could have called him "Rocky" and meant a foundation stone. It seems more likely that the incident is a sample of Our Lord's sense of humor. He meant the nickname to be taken as a joke, the way close friends will call a fat man "skinny." In any case, the first disciples were charmed. They were drawn to Jesus because of the very warm and human way He approached them, seeking them out on their own down-to-earth level.

## 2.

Our Lord was after Peter. This is the chief element in everybody's vocation. There are not many men who listen to Jesus the first time when He says, "Come and follow me," and drop everything and follow Him. In the Synoptic Gospels it *sounds* that way, but remember that the Synoptics are a *kerygma*, that is, a sort of catechism or abridged C.C.D. course, a summary of Our Lord's teaching, which the apostles preached to live congregations. They did not try to include all the details. If you study the Gospels carefully, you see that the disciples had a lot of contact with Jesus and witnessed many miracles before they finally came around and made a final commitment. They really had known Him quite a while before He even asked them to make such a commitment. This is the normal way human things work. The evangelists are just summarizing when they simply say: "Jesus saw the sons of Zebedee in a boat, called them, and they immediately dropped their nets and followed Him."

They followed Him that day no doubt. But as regards any kind of permanent commitment, that took some persuading and a lot of time.

Jesus was on Peter's trail. He wanted to make something out of him. One day Jesus was passing along the Lake of Galilee, where Peter had his business, and called him out of the boat. Peter followed Him that day, and from then on began visiting Jesus more often and staying longer. He started following Him around the countryside. He saw Him change water into wine at the marriage feast of Cana. To put it briefly, they were getting acquainted.

One day Jesus came to Capernaum, Simon Peter's town, and went into *his* house. This was a significant choice. It was a small town. You know what it means if a celebrity—and Jesus was beginning to get a name for Himself—comes to *your* town and stays at *your* house. It means something.

Now there was a little problem with the serving. Peter's mother-in-law was ill and in bed. Jesus took her by the hand and cured her so that she could serve the guests. Peter must have appreciated this prompt way of solving his difficulty. Then, towards the end of the day, everybody from the town and the surrounding countryside brought the sick and laid them at Peter's doorstep. Jesus cured them all. Well, for a citizen of a small town, this was all very flattering. It was beginning to build Peter up. He was really getting interested.

Then Jesus silently stole away for a night of prayer in the desert. He was probably tired out after all that activity. Who is the one to go in search of Him? Peter, of course.

Peter's leadership qualities begin to emerge. I suspect that in our day Peter would have been president of the local Rotary Club.

Apparently a meeting of important people in the town had been held and it was decided to send a delegation of distinguished citizens to get Jesus back. He had worked so many miracles. He had cured so many sick people. The town had suddenly acquired something really outstanding. "We must not let this man get away!"

Since Jesus had worked all these miracles at Peter's house, eaten his supper there and cured the sick at his doorstep, the citizens decided that Peter was just the man to go and find Him and bring Him back. Or perhaps it was Peter himself who said, "I'm the man for the job." In any case, Peter led the delegation "in pursuit of Jesus."

Peter marched out into the desert to get his man and bring Him back. He found Jesus in prayer. As He turned to greet Peter, those eyes of His must have had a quizzical expression in them. Peter, losing a little bit of his steam, exclaimed, "Everybody is looking for you!" Our Lord's reply was striking, "Let us go some place else."

"Let *us*," that is, *you* and *me*, "go some place else." In other words, "I am not interested in the fact that everybody is seeking me. I am interested in whether *you* are seeking me." It is like that incident a little later when Our Lord will call His disciples aside and ask them, "Who do men say that I am?" And after they offer various answers, He asks more pointedly, "But who do *you* say that I am?"

Our Lord was saying to Peter, "I know you are enthused about me. I know you want me back there. But you have a whole lot of motives for this that do not interest me at all. I

am interested in *you*, Peter, as a person, not what all these
other people want me to do."

### 3.

One day Jesus was preaching near the shore of the lake.
A huge crowd was surging all around Him so that He had
scarcely enough room in which to breathe. There were
several boats lying close to the shore. Jesus got into Peter's
boat and preached from there. Having finished His talk to
the people, He said to Simon, "Put out into the deep, and
have your men lower the nets for a haul."

Notice the delicacy of Our Lord's request. This was no
big business that Peter was boss of, and when later on he
boasted, "We have left *everything* and followed you," it
was a lot of baloney. He had only two small boats and a
couple of hired men. But Our Lord spoke to him as you
would speak to somebody who is a big executive: "Ask
your men to lower the nets."

Peter remonstrated. He was a successful fisherman and
thought he knew his business. "Master," he said, "you are
a teacher by profession. We don't expect you to know
much about fishing. For one thing, we have labored all
night and caught nothing. Besides, the fish on this particular lake do not bite at all during the day."

In other words, "You know *your* business, and I know
*mine*....However, to satisfy you, we'll let down the nets
once again."

Thus Peter graciously condescended to Our Lord's request. So the men set to their oars, went out into the
middle of the lake and let down the nets. All at once, to
their astonishment, the nets started tightening. Then they
began to bulge. The boat started tipping to one side. The
men yelled to their companions in the other boat to come

and help them. John and James were in business with them. They hastened out in their boat. There was such an extraordinary number of fish in this single haul that the nets were threatening to break. In the end both boats were so filled with fish that they were on the point of sinking.

This was the kind of miracle that would impress any fisherman!—especially after having labored all night and caught nothing.

When Peter saw what had happened, his eyes got bigger and bigger and bigger. Suddenly he threw himself at Our Lord's feet. He was used to giving orders to his two or three hired men, and to his mother-in-law. True to style, he blurted out, "Lord, leave my boat, for I am a sinful man!" He was so excited and thrilled, he did not know just what he was saying.

"A feeling of awe had gripped him, as it had all of his associates, because of the number of fish caught in the haul."

The event settled Peter's mind. The miraculous haul of fish was his definitive call to become a disciple of Jesus. It was the kind of approach that went straight to his heart, which suited his personality, his life circumstances, even his business. It was the moment of grace.

The Gospel tells us that when they brought the boats to shore, Peter, James, and John abandoned everything and became His followers. This is the moment they really were converted and became full-time followers. Before this they had followed Him once in a while or for a few days at a time. Now there was a permanent commitment. From this time on, Our Lord began to train them in His school of apostolic formation. It was a real novitiate. Our Lord worked on the disciples for the next two or three years, with a great deal of failure as well as success.

### 4.

Among the many miracles that occurred soon after, there is one which is particularly impressive, the raising of Jairus' daughter who was only twelve. When Jesus was told that she had already died, He said to the father, "You have nothing to fear; only have faith that she will be safe."

Our Lord always recommended faith to those who did not have it and praised it whenever He found it.

When Jesus arrived at the home of the little girl, He would not allow anyone to enter the house with Him except Peter, James and John. He threw out all the professional mourners and, taking the little girl by the hand, raised her to life. To be a specially chosen witness of this astonishing miracle was a fact not lost on Peter.

A little later, Jesus chose twelve apostles from among his disciples and gave them a mission. He told them to go into all the towns and villages that He planned to visit. "I give you power to cast out demons and to heal the sick," He said to them. "Tell them the kingdom of heaven is at hand."

So they went off on their mission. Demons were driven out in droves; people were cured of all kinds of diseases; the whole thing was a smashing success. They were pleased with themselves as well as with the results of their mission.

As soon as they returned, Jesus gathered them together, and for the sake of privacy, withdrew to an out-of-the-way place for a period of rest and prayer. When they had calmed down, He said to them: "Don't be so full of joy over all the miraculous powers you exercised, but rather rejoice because your names are written in heaven."

In this way, He gently put the lid on their excessive enthusiasm for what is really secondary. The main thing is that their names are written in heaven, which might be paraphrased, "You have been called by my Father. That's the great thing about you. He loves you. And these wonders you have been able to do, well, fine if you can do them. But do not get too excited about them."

Then comes the miracle of the multiplication of the loaves and fishes. A huge crowd had gathered to hear Jesus. It was getting late and the apostles were worried. "We had better send everybody home," they said.

But Jesus replied, "No, pass out the bread and fish that you have."

The disciples started passing out the food, and as they did, to their great amazement, the bread and fish began multiplying in their hands. We speak today about active participation in the liturgy, but here was active participation in a miracle! You can imagine what a state of mind Peter was in. After being singled out to be one of the three to see the little girl raised from the dead; after his success on the mission of the apostles; and now active participation in the miracle of the loaves! He must have been just about floating! This is what might be called one of his "up" periods.

5.

Our Lord likes to alternate "ups" and "downs." So, shortly afterwards comes a "down." We might call it, "The Dunking of Peter." Perhaps Our Lord thought the best way to cool his ardor was to send him for a swim.

After the miracle of the multiplication of the loaves and fishes, Jesus had retired to a mountain to pray. The disciples got into a boat and on His instructions started rowing across the lake.

"Jesus obliged them to proceed to the other shore ahead of Him, while He dismissed the crowd Himself and went

off to pray alone. During the last part of the night, He
came toward them, walking over the sea."

When they saw this figure walking on the sea, they were
scared. They cried out, "It's a ghost!"

He called back, "Don't be afraid. Take heart. It is I."

There it was, this vision coming towards them, walking
on the water. And here they were, in the boat, bouncing
around in the waves. When Our Lord called out, "Don't be
afraid," these words resounded like a trumpet call to
Peter's pride. He did not want to be rated with these other
guys. "Lord, tell me (once again the commanding tone) to
come to you over the water!"

The Lord replied, "Come ahead."

Peter climbed over the edge of the boat, his eyes fixed on
the Lord, and started moving in the direction of Jesus. He
*was* walking over the water!

Suddenly, he began to feel the stiff wind against his
cheeks. He took alarm! Then he saw those big waves. He
was terrified! He began to sink. But he had enough
presence of mind to cry out, "Lord, save me!"

This was what Jesus was waiting for. Immediately He
reached out His hand and pulled him out of the dark
water. Our Lord climbed into the boat, while the others
dragged in the poor, waterlogged fisherman. Peter looked
like a drowned rat. This switch of roles from fisherman to
fish must have been humiliating for him, especially in the
presence of his friends.

Jesus gives us a good lesson in spiritual direction in this
incident. There are some people to whom you can never
tell anything. The only way they can learn is from experience. If you try to tell them, "Look, if you bang your head
against a stone wall, you'll get a big lump and a headache,
and here are the reasons why,"—they will not listen to

you. You can give them all kinds of reasons from science or theology, but they will not believe you. The only way for them to learn is to bang their heads against the wall, feel the bump, and get the headache. From then on, they will agree with you, but not before.

Peter's friends, who were wise to him, were delighted to witness his discomfiture. They did not hesitate to remind him that he made an excellent fisherman, but not much of a fish.

Our Lord could have said to him, "Look, Peter, for goodness sake, cool it, will you? Stay in the boat like the others!" But instead, Our Lord took him seriously and said, "Come on."

When Peter had dried his hair, and perhaps his tears, Jesus remarked, "Peter, how little faith you have!" This rebuke implies that Peter *could* have walked on the water—it's all the same to Our Lord. By pointing out to Peter how little faith he had, Jesus made him reflect on his motivation. Maybe he was not so much in love with Our Lord as he thought. Maybe love was not the motive for getting out of the boat. If that had been the motive, he would have succeeded. But he was trying to pull himself up by his own bootstraps; or to put it another way, he was trying to get ahead of grace and to make a big impression on his companions. And so Our Lord let him fall on his face.

That is what will happen to us every time we start sticking our chests out a little too far or trying to impress people. Our Lord lets us trip over something and down we go. Then it is time to pray, frankly acknowledge our fault, and wait for God's healing grace.

When they reached the shore, the crowd which had been fed miraculously by Our Lord was waiting for them. In

answer to their questions, Jesus launched into a long discourse on faith and the Eucharist, which brought about a
parting of the ways. Many walked away from Jesus for
good. John tells us that He turned to His disciples and said,
"Will you also go away?"

They replied, "No, we'll stick by you." Peter was their
spokesman. Our Lord appreciated this vote of confidence
very much, because even some of His own disciples said
goodbye and went back home. The teaching about the
Eucharist was too much for them.

Every now and then a crisis like this occurred in the life
of Our Lord's disciples, and they had to make a decision.
This was one of those important and decisive moments,
and Peter wound up on the right side.

### 6.

A certain matter was bothering the disciples at this time,
Peter especially. This was the fact that Our Lord leveled
reproaches and severe criticism at the leaders of the Jewish
people, that is, at the big shots. "These Pharisees are blind
guides...I'm going to root up all these plants and throw
them out."

The disciples came to Him after one of these sessions and
complained, "Gee, Lord, the Pharisees did not like what
you said at all. If you are to be accepted by them as the
Messiah, don't you think it would be better to speak a little
less frankly?"

The disciples had a lot of stock invested in Our Lord's
political success. They conceived of Him as the Messiah in
the sense of a national hero and king. They were
concerned about His career. He constantly tried to break
them of this narrow-minded idea, but they did not understand what Our Lord was talking about. In fact, this lack

of comprehension was characteristic of them. Mark tells us that after the miraculous multiplication of loaves and the discourse on the Eucharist, the minds of the disciples "were a perfect blank." They did not understand what it all meant.

On one great occasion, when Our Lord thought it was time, He turned to Peter and asked: "Who do you say that I am?"

People were saying this and that about Him. It was at this moment that Peter made his great act of faith: "You are Christ, the Son of the Living God!"

Our Lord rewarded him by saying, "Peter, on you I will build my Church."

This was a great promise, greater indeed than the promise made to Abraham, Isaac, and Jacob. But He said, "I will build my Church on you." He did not say, "I am giving you the Church now."

Noticing Peter's chest beginning to bulge just a little bit, He added quickly, "Now do not tell anybody about this." Peter would have liked to have called in the photographers. Peter had a secret desire (not too secret from the others) to be the right-hand man of the Messiah. He had convinced himself that this was his proper role. When Jesus recognized that Peter was taking his future mission too seriously, and in merely human terms, He began to speak to Peter and the apostles about His passion and death.

"From that time, Jesus began to make it plain to the disciples that it was necessary that He go up to Jerusalem, suffer at the hands of the elders, high priest, and scribes, die, and on the third day rise again."

In other words, this kingdom of His was to be established not by political power, ambition, or prestige, but by suffering and the Cross. Peter had to change his ideas about what the head of the apostolic college meant.

### 7.

Peter was still concerned about the attitude of the scribes and Pharisees—things were not going too well in that important area of public opinion. The next scene is really astonishing. It shows us how matter of fact and how much at ease the disciples were with Our Lord. For, as incredible as it might seem, Peter called Jesus aside *to lecture Him.* That is what the Gospel says: "Peter drew Him aside and proceeded to lecture"—the Son of God!

He said, "Lord, this business of going up to Jerusalem and being crucified—I don't think it is such a hot idea. The scribes and Pharisees have shown disapproval of the way things are going, and they have been offended by your remarks. Now you are speaking about being crucified. What will happen to the Messianic Kingdom? What will happen to *us*?" *What will happen to Peter!*

And his final admonition was, "May God spare you, Master . . . Let's not talk any more about suffering, please!"

Although He had just made him the chief of the apostles, the Lord turned on him angrily and said: "Back to your place, Satan!" A stinging rebuke! The other disciples heard it and trembled. Our Lord said it loud enough so that they would all hear. He turned on Peter the full force of His indignation, because now Peter was meddling in something essential to the kingdom, the Will of the Father. For without the Cross, there is no salvation. Our Lord was willing to take his commands—up to a point—but not in something essential. "Get out of my sight!"

"Satan"—that's about as bad a word as He could call him—"You are a stumbling block."

You can see Peter beginning to shrivel up. "You do not take God's view of things, but man's."

Our Lord knows how to administer a rebuke, to put somebody in his place, from the top man to the lowest. When we have moved out of our territory, He lets us know about it in no uncertain terms.

That humiliation must have really hurt Peter. The words of Jesus must have pierced through him like a two-edged sword, right to the bottom of his heart. He did not have any comeback.

But Our Lord was not satisfied with that. He turned on the other disciples ready to get rid of them, too, if they would not accept the doctrine of the Cross.

"Look," He said, "if anyone wants to become my follower, let him deny himself and shoulder his cross. Only then may he be a follower of mine. Somebody who is bent on saving his life is going to part with it anyway. He who freely parts with his life for my sake will save it and secure it in the end. What does it profit a man if he gains the whole world, and loses his own soul?"

Our Lord really gave it to Peter on that occasion. Peter was really flattened. He needed some consolation. Notice how Our Lord responds. He had given him a blow right between the eyes, and now He gives him a big consolation. The harder we fall, the higher we bounce.

### 8.

Now comes the event called the Transfiguration—an overwhelming consolation for any man if there ever was one. Again, Jesus calls to Himself Peter, James and John, and they go up onto a high mountain. Jesus is transfigured before them. The glory that lay concealed in the depths of His soul started to stream down over His body. His face shone like the sun, and even His clothes took on an unbelievably beautiful glow, like snow sparkling in the sunshine. Suddenly Moses and Elias appeared together with Him, talking to Him about His death, which He was about to undergo in Jerusalem. The apostles were thrilled, of course, with the vision. The beauty filled their senses and their hearts with warm emotion. They wanted to linger there on the mountain and enjoy to the full the delightful feelings of consolation that seemed to penetrate to the very marrow of their bones.

Peter, as usual, had to say something. Silence was never one of his virtues. "Lord, it is well that we are here with you. If you would like, we will build three tents: one for you, one for Moses, and one for Elias."

Very hospitable of Peter to devise these special accommodations for Jesus and His guests, something no one had asked him to do.

While he was still speaking, a luminous cloud enveloped them, and a voice rang out: "This is My beloved Son in Whom I am well pleased. Listen to Him."

They fell on their faces, trembling, overcome with awe. After a while Jesus approached them. They were still scared to death and would not get up. But when He laid His hand on them and patted them, they looked up and saw only Him.

The afterglow of that vision must have been tremendous. As they came down the mountain, Peter began to recover from his astonishment and awe. He was thinking how nice it would be to tell all the other disciples about the wonderful vision he had just enjoyed. How highly they would esteem him as one of the inside men!

Jesus turned to him and said, "There is one thing I want to add, Peter. Do not tell anybody about this vision until I have risen from the dead."

Jesus was always gently putting the lid on Peter's exuberance, but He did it in such a way as never to squash him.

9.

Peter was in one of his "up" periods following the Transfiguration. He was, in fact, way up. For that very reason, he was in danger of a new and painful fall. Jesus took this occasion to make a little test: He spoke of His passion a second time. While they were wandering around in Galilee, Jesus said to the apostles: "The Son of Man is going to be betrayed into the hands of men. They will put Him to death, but on the third day, He will rise again."

They were all exceedingly distressed. This time Peter made no comment. He had learned his lesson; he was silent. But another humiliation was in store for him.

Jesus and His followers entered Capernaum, and along came a tax collector. He interviewed Peter, who evidently was representing himself as the spokesman for this delegation, and asked him, "Does not your Rabbi pay the temple dues?" (Everybody, of course, paid the temple dues.) Peter promptly replied, "Of course, our Master pays the temple dues! We always pay our dues. We are law-abiding citizens!" Any slur on the Master was a slur on Peter, too.

Then he went indoors, and before he could say a word, Jesus called him to His side: "Let me have a word with you, Simon. What do you think, on whom do earthly sovereigns levy taxes, on their own children, or on outsiders?"

Peter was beginning to get a little uneasy about this conversation. Jesus was the Son of God. Obviously His heavenly Father owned the Temple. As God's Son, He could hardly be expected to pay taxes on His Father's

House. Peter had to answer the question the only way it could be answered: "On outsiders."

Jesus continued, "Then the children are exempt."

In other words: "Who do you think you are, committing me, not just yourself, to pay the temple dues?"

Once again Jesus asks a searching question to get Peter to enter into his motivation and to ask himself the "why." This is Peter in the raw. We see him in his predominant fault, human respect, the fault which later led him to deny Jesus three times.

First Peter says the "right thing" to please the tax collector. Then he says the "right thing" to please Jesus. That puts him in a dilemma: "I have said that my Master pays the tax. But I see now that Jesus does not have to pay the tax..."

Peter was beginning to sweat. He is really on the frying pan. Once again, his impetuosity has gotten him into trouble. As usual he had spoken up too soon. He should have gone in and consulted Jesus first. He was not in charge of anything. That was the point Jesus wanted to make. Our Lord had said, "Peter, on you I *will* build my Church," that is, in the future. Jesus did not give him any mandate that *day*. So poor Peter was really chagrined.

Our Lord graciously gets him off the hook. "However," He went on to say, and you can see Our Lord smiling, "we must not give them any offense," putting His finger squarely on Peter's problem. "Here is what you can do. Go down to the sea, throw in a hook, and grab the first fish that you come up with. Look in its mouth and you will find the coin to pay the tax. Take that to the tax collector for you and for me."

These words are full of humor and gentle irony. First of all, Peter is a big time fisherman with nets, not a hook. He has to go down to the shore, put a little bait on a hook, drop it in, sit there, and wait. And it becomes more and more obvious to him as time goes by that the first fish to come along is going to be a symbol of himself, someone who can't keep his big mouth shut. The first fish that comes along does in fact have the necessary funds in its *big* mouth. The other disciples, who have followed him down to the shore to see how he made out, were not bashful about egging him on and congratulating him. This is Peter in all his delightful humanness, and Jesus in His.

### 10.

Peter is now in one of his "down" periods. The sons of Zebedee thought that this might be a good time to press their ambitious claims. They persuaded their mother to suggest to Jesus that they have the top places in the approaching Messianic Kingdom. Accordingly, the mother of the sons of Zebedee came and prostrated herself in front of Jesus saying, "I have this favor to ask of you."

Our Lord said, "What is your request?"

"Grant that these, my two sons, may sit with you, one on the right, the other on the left, in your kingdom."

You can see the blood starting to boil in the other disciples. "Why, these two sons of…!" And who was more indignant than Peter to see his two former partners trying to make off with the two top places in the kingdom?

Our Lord does not reply to her. He turns to the boys: "Look, do you realize what you are asking? Can you drink the cup that I will drink?"

Over and over again in the Gospel, Our Lord asks pointed questions. He does not usually tell people what is wrong with them, or that they are doing something stupid. He asks them a question that makes them look into their own inner motives and judge themselves.

The sons of Zebedee reply, "Yes, we can drink it."

Jesus' comment on this was, "Yes, you will drink my cup, but what you are asking for, I cannot give, because those places have been reserved for whomever my Father wants there."

Thus Our Lord gently, but firmly, puts them in their place.

And as soon as they were in their place, the other disciples became indignant towards the two brothers. Jesus then gave them all an important lesson on what authority is in His Kingdom. "He who wants to be prince among you must be your servant, and he who would be a leader among you has got to be the slave of all."

In other words, "You have just got a totally wrong idea about what having the first place means."

### 11.

Peter is still a bit down, so Jesus gives him a little boost. He sends him to prepare the paschal supper. Events are coming to a quick conclusion now, and Jesus has got His bitter passion to go through. He selected Peter for the job, but just so he would not think he was the only person in the show, Jesus sent John along to help him. So Peter and John go off to prepare the supper.

When everything has been arranged and all are reclining at table, Jesus interrupts the supper to wash the feet of the apostles. Here again we see Peter in his characteristic faults. Our Lord wants to give an example. He wants to do something for Peter and the others. He wants to serve them. He goes around to each and, like a slave, washes their feet. When He comes to Peter, Peter says, "Oh no! Wash *my* feet? Never!" It is his usual speech before he thinks.

Our Lord says quietly and firmly, "What I want to do,

you do not understand. But will you please let me wash your feet? You will understand it by and by."

A lot of people are like Peter. You cannot do anything for them. They have always got to do something for you. But sometimes Our Lord wants to do something for us. We may not realize *why* He is doing it, but we can be sure He is not doing it for nothing.

Jesus warns, "If I do not wash these feet of yours, you will have no part with me."

Then Peter goes from one extreme to the other: "Wash my head, my hands, everything!"

If you or I had been Our Lord, I think we would have taken that basin and...Our Lord remains calm, puts up with Peter, and finally succeeds in washing his feet.

During the last supper, there is another row over who is going to be the greatest. Even up to the last moments of Our Lord's life, the disciples cannot seem to get it through their heads what discipleship really means.

Jesus tries to prepare them for His going away and for His passion, but without much success. They are like little children gathered around their father who is trying to explain some great family tragedy to them. They just cannot understand; it is too much for them. Our Lord goes out of His way. He stoops to the farthest possible extent to explain His going away to them, but He finally has to give up. Later, they will understand.

He had warned them, "You are all going to be shaken in your faith, because it is written: 'I will strike the shepherd, and the sheep of the flock will be scattered.' But after I am risen from the dead (notice that He always encourages them, gives them hope), I will go before you to Galilee, and there you will see me."

Here Peter speaks up: "Even if all the others lose faith in you, I will not be shaken in mine."

This is Peter at his impetuous best. He is like some giant missile about to take off from the launching pad with great billows of smoke and an ear-splitting blast—but nothing happens; it remains on the ground, just a big fizzle.

Jesus replied, "I have to be plain with you, Peter. This night before the cock crows, you will deny me three times."

Peter said, "Even if I die with you, I will never disown you." He is confident of himself, quite sure of his own loyalty and reliability, instead of trusting in God's help and protection. He never learned that lesson during Our Lord's earthly ministry. So Our Lord leaves it there. Peter will have to learn by experience.

### 12.

During the course of Our Lord's passion, Peter not only goes to sleep in the garden but is no help or consolation whatsoever. He even makes a fool of himself and embarrasses Our Lord by cutting off the ear of the high priest's servant. Then he seems to have run away. Later, he shows up, standing in back of the Praetorium warming himself by a fire. When he is confronted and challenged by the servant girl, he disowns Our Lord once, twice, a third time. The last time, the servant girl says to him, "You are one of them! Your accent betrays you."

Bursting out cursing and swearing—he has not forgotten how to do that—Peter shouts, "I have nothing to do with that man!"

This is the great Peter, the would-be right-hand-man of the Messiah, the one who was going to die for Him; the one who was going to do all sorts of things for Jesus; the one who had "given up everything to follow Him." When the chips were down, so was he. Immediately, a cock crows. What a gong that must have sounded in Peter's ears! He remembered the prediction of the Master, "Before a cock crows, you will disown me three times." He went out and wept bitterly. In Luke's account, we are told that Our Lord looked at him, their eyes met, and it was after that that Peter went out and broke into sobs.

Think how Peter felt when he looked into those eyes. It was the darkest hour of his life. For the first time he realized: "I am not worthy to be a disciple of Jesus Christ." And he just could not stand himself anymore. He went out, and wept his heart out. He realized for the first time that of himself he was nothing: just a total failure, a lot of hot air. One look from Our Lord. . . .

When Jesus really wants to make something out of us, He looks at us in the way He looked at Peter. He makes us see into the depths of our own hearts and perceive how much evil is there under so many disguises. In that moment when Jesus looked at Peter, he stripped him of all his pretenses and disguises.

Our Lord had to go on alone, with no help from Peter or the other apostles. He had to go through the work of the Redemption alone and lay down His life for them. Only after it was over, did they start reviving, and only because He revived them.

Peter, because of his triple denial, was in the deepest depression of them all. With His usual touching thoughtfulness, in His very first appearance after His Resurrection, Jesus sent Peter a special message. He said to the women at the empty tomb, "Go tell the disciples *and Peter* that I have risen." As Peter gradually revived, it was a new Peter, much-chastened, much wiser.

## 13.

The most important appearance of Jesus after His resurrection, as far as Peter was concerned, occurred by the Lake of Tiberius. Our Lord had said to the disciples, "Go to Galilee, I will meet you there." So they went to Galilee and were sitting around, waiting. They waited, and waited some more. They finally got tired of waiting. Peter, more restless than all the others, announced: "I am going fishing." As if to say, "No use sitting around here any longer—nothing is happening."

The others said, "Okay. We will go with you." They got into the boat, rowed out into the lake, and started fishing.

The night wore on. It got later, and later, and later. Nothing happened. It was one of those fishless nights—a vivid symbol of what we feel when we have been praying for something a long time and nothing happens. We ask and ask, but no reply comes. They were out on the lake the whole night. Their frustration and annoyance were mounting as the night drew to a close.

Towards dawn, a stranger appeared on the shore and called out to them, "Lads, have you caught anything?"

They looked at one another with a mounting indignation. "Who does this guy think he is?" Anybody should know that fishermen would not be out there at that time of the night if they had caught anything at all.

So they yelled back, "No!"

Not to be put off by their unfriendly reply to his friendly greeting, the stranger called back, "Why not cast your net over to the other side of the boat? Then you will catch something."

They had nothing to lose, so they cast the net on the other side of the boat and immediately there was a tremendous catch. This set of circumstances is remarkably similar to that described on the occasion of Peter's first call to discipleship.

John, at once, recognizes who the Stranger is, and says to Peter, "That must be the Lord!"

John, the Beloved Disciple, had the perception that comes from love and instantly recognizes Our Lord in the event. This is what characterizes a living faith. It penetrates the events of life and recognizes Our Lord in them.

Peter, in characteristic fashion, jumps into the water and swims ashore. Our Lord says, "I have everything under control." He had thoughtfully begun to fry some fish for the hungry fishermen. He said to Peter, "Why don't you go and count the fish? Afterwards bring me some fish from those you have caught."

The others, meanwhile, were taking their time. They had brought the fish ashore and were sorting them out.

The Gospel says, "They gathered around Jesus for breakfast." He had invited them, saying, "Come, and eat." But no one dared to ask Who He was. They knew Who He was.

Their meal is something like our meal with Jesus in the Eucharist. There are no external exchanges, but there is real communication, an exchange that is all interior and too deep for words. Jesus is gradually preparing them for a new kind of presence that they do not know about yet, which will be given them through the outpouring of the Holy Spirit at Pentecost.

### 14.

They finished their breakfast, and then Our Lord called Peter aside. They walked together down the beach. Jesus put His arm around him. But Peter's heart sank, three times. Perhaps he was thinking, "Well, I guess this is it. I denied the Lord three times. Now He is going to remind me of my denials, and tell me that John is going to take over as top man."

The expectation of this inevitable confrontation had been lying heavy on Peter's mind. He does not speak up during any of the apparitions of the Risen Christ which precede this one. He was too crushed after his triple denial to say anything. He knew that he had failed, and that it was right that John should take over. He, Peter, was no darn good. It was only right that Jesus should look around for somebody better. No one could have done any worse than he: to deny the Lord three times.

Jesus had permitted those three serious sins in order to let Peter come to know himself. Now He intended to put the finishing touches to the job. So He said to Peter, using his given name and speaking in a very formal manner, "Simon, son of John, do you love me?" The word that Our Lord used means supernatural love, charity, disinterested love, the love that lasts forever. "Do you *love* me?"

Peter replies, "Lord, you know that I love you." But he does not use the word for love which the Lord has just used. The word Peter uses is the love of one person for another, human love.

This is the first time Peter has taken full stock of himself. All he can lay claim to is that he loves Our Lord as a friend loves a friend. He does not lay claim to anything higher.

Our Lord replies, "Feed my lambs."

At first glance, it seems as though Our Lord is offering Peter a chance to atone for his triple denial by a triple act of love. But on closer observation, something more profound seems to be taking place in this exchange. The Lord, by means of these searching, excruciating questions, is literally lifting Peter and hurling him from one abyss of humiliation to another. All those other humiliations were nothing compared to these. He is talking heart-to-heart to Peter, and putting His finger on the thing that is most precious and deep in him—his love for Him—and *calling it into question.* He is deliberately doubting it.

"He said to him a second time, 'Simon, son of John, do you really love me?' "

Again, Jesus speaks of charity, disinterested love. "Do you really love me in the way I showed you when I died for you, and in the way I commanded you and the other disciples to show love for one another?"

Peter does not want to risk claiming anything, so he replies using the same words as before, "I do love you with my human affection."

The Lord answers, "Be shepherd of my flock."

Peter is becoming aware that he is being reinstated as head of the apostles. But at what a price! The price is utter humiliation! This is the goal of all Our Lord's formation: Humility. It alone leads to the love He is talking about.

Now comes the final question: "Simon, son of John (and here He uses Peter's own word), do you *really* love me— even *with your human affection?* Are you *really* my friend?" This must have hurt. In other words, "Are you even sure of your human affection for me?" Or again, "Do you really love me *at all?*"

Peter is spiritually naked before Jesus with his poor, wretched and miserable humanity. He has nothing to offer except what Jesus is giving him. Our Lord rewards him for each new humiliation as he accepts it with a towering height of grace, confirming him in his unique vocation as the "rock," turning this heap of sand into a solid block of granite on which to build His Church.

The Gospel says that it "grieved" Peter that He asked him a third time, "Do you really love me at all?"

Peter cries out in desperation, "Lord, you *know* everything," appealing to His divine knowledge. But then, as if fearing what this divine judgment might be, he returns to his appeal to Jesus' human knowledge, repeating for the third time, "You know (just from human observation) that I love you!"

His affirmation is still only in terms of human affection, as if to say, "Won't you please believe in my poor human love for you?"

Absolutely humbled before Our Lord and those standing around them, Peter heard Our Lord say, "Feed my sheep...I make you the chief of the apostles because of your lowliness, which you now fully accept. I am going to give you the heroic love that you do not dare to lay claim to. One day you will indeed lay down your life for me."

His last words to Peter are the same as the very first words He spoke to him long ago: "Follow me."

These are the same words Jesus had spoken to him when He called him out of his boat. But what a difference! What depths of meaning they have acquired over the years! The same voice, the same words. The ears which hear are the same. But the heart has been transfigured. We, too, have to start out to follow Him again and again, no matter how far we may have advanced.

This is the great Apostle whom Jesus made with His own hands. And Jesus is taking us up with the same gentleness and firmness, and leading us in the same direction. What He is ultimately asking of any apostle is not what he has done, but whether he loves Him.

"*Do you really love me*?" Peter's answer to that question is what makes a true apostle.

# XVIII.  LAZARUS: Symbol of Christian Awakening

The story of Lazarus is a preview of Jesus' approaching death and resurrection. Lazarus stands for fallen man about to be raised from the death of sin to life in God through Christ's Passion, Death, and Resurrection. The illness which Jesus allows Lazarus to undergo is the symbol of Man's false self with all its weakness, ignorance, and pride, together with all the damage lying in the unconscious from earliest childhood to the present moment. To raise Lazarus from this illness to life in the Spirit is the most profound meaning of the event. Lazarus' resurrection manifests the full significance of Christ's resurrection, which restores sinful humanity, not only to the divine Life, but to its superabounding fullness.

Jesus hints at the special character of Lazarus' illness in these words: "This illness will not result in death, but will promote the glory of God." Lazarus represents in a special way those who seek to penetrate the mystery of Christ to its depths. This disposition is manifested by a willingness to die to the false self and to wait in patience for the inner resurrection, which can only come from Christ.

1.

"A man named Lazarus was ill. He was at Bethany, the village where Mary and her sister were living. Mary is that person who anointed the Lord's feet with perfume and wiped them with her hair. It was her brother Lazarus that was ill.

"So the sisters sent Him this message: 'Please, Master, your dear friend is ill.'

"When receiving the news, Jesus said: 'This illness will not result in death. No, it is to promote the glory of God. Through it, the Son of God is to be glorified.'

"Now Jesus loved Martha and her sister and Lazarus. So when He learned that he was ill, He tarried, it is true, for two days in the place where He was."[1]

Lazarus' illness was that special kind of illness that God sends to His friends. What did Lazarus think when Jesus did not come? Or the sisters, as they watched Lazarus slowly wasting away? They had sent Jesus a message about the seriousness of his illness. They knew that Jesus loved Lazarus—and loved *them*. He had made their home a stopping-off place on His many journeys to Jerusalem, and a place of rest after teaching in the Temple during the day. John himself, in describing this event, seems astonished that Jesus did not hasten to come at once. He writes, half apologetically, "He tarried, it is true"—as if to say, "I must admit"—two extra days after receiving the information. He apparently ignored His friend's request and the anguish of the sisters. By staying away two more days, He not only allowed the illness to get worse, but allowed Lazarus to undergo death, and possibly even corruption. Lazarus was in the tomb four days before Jesus finally arrived.

What is this mysterious illness that comes upon those whom Jesus loves in a special way? It is the recognition of the false self, which comprises all the evil habits that have been woven into our personality from the time we were conceived. It includes the emotional damage that may have come from our upbringing and environment; all the harm that other people have done to us, knowingly or unknowingly, at an age when we could not defend ourselves; and all the methods we acquired, many of them now unconscious, to ward off the pain of unbearable situations. This mass of human misery is a significant part of the sufferings of the illness.

Actually, Lazarus had always been sick, but without being aware of it. The illness consisted of his becoming *aware* that he was sick and in having the illness run its full course, ending in the death of his false self. Only then could God, through the power of the Holy Spirit, raise him to the fullness of life, which is the fruit (here anticipated) of Christ's death and resurrection.

The story of Lazarus' falling ill and dying is in line with the scriptural texts which manifest the trials and inner feelings of God's friends in the face of the experience of their sinfulness. They may not have contributed anything in the way of personal guilt. It was just the weight of original sin and its consequences at work in their lives. This sheer misery is the object of God's purifying action both in them and in us. The divine light begins to shine in our souls with such intensity that we are able to perceive clearly just how sick we really are.

If we were sitting in a dimly lit room that seemed to be well swept and respectable, and some one should turn on fifty 1,000 watt bulbs, the place would start to crawl. This is what happens interiorly when God turns up the voltage of His inner light. Then, even one who feels he has been great friends with God, may begin to wonder whether he has ever heard of God. Job described his experience in these words: "What crime, what wrongdoing is mine? Why is it that thou turnest thy back on me, and treat me as an enemy? As well wrestle with a flying leaf, chase a wisp of straw, as keep this jealous record against me, tax me with the offences of my youth! To hold me so close a prisoner, watch me wherever I go, track my footprints, when I am no better than rotting carrion, than a garment fretted away by the moth!"[2]

Two extremes meet in this illness: the divine light and human misery. The soul melts away in the presence of God. It feels its spiritual substance demolished and cries out in the words of Psalm 69: "O God, save me; see how the waters close about me, threatening my life. I am like one who sticks in the deep mire, no ground under his feet; hoarse my throat with crying wearily for help. My eyes ache looking for the mercy of God."[3]

Perhaps the most poignant of all the aspects of this experience is the confrontation between the majesty of God and the dire spiritual poverty of the person who is becoming aware of how sick he really is. Jonah experienced this as rejection, as he prayed in the belly of the whale: "Here in the depths of the sea's heart you would cast me away, all the flood of your waves are sweeping over me, till it seems as if I were shut out from your regard."[4]

Another characteristic symptom of this illness is the conviction of being punished, imprisoned, abandoned, and that God is refusing to hear one's desperate cries for help. To quote Jeremiah, the Prophet: "Ah, what straits have I not known, under the avenging rod! I asked for light and into ever deeper shadows the Lord's guidance led me. Always upon me, none other, falls endlessly the blow. Broken this frame under the wrinkled skin, the sunk flesh. Bitterness of despair fills my prospect, walled in on every side. Buried in darkness and, like the dead, interminably. Closely He fences me in, beyond hope of rescue; loads me with fetters. Cry out for mercy as I will, prayer of mine wins no audience. Climb these smooth walls I may not; every way of escape He has undone."⁵

This is what Lazarus was feeling when he realized that Jesus could have come and healed him, and did not come. The illness had to run its full course in order to accomplish its purpose, for there is no way it can be accomplished except by going through it. That is why, having heard how ill Lazarus was, "Jesus tarried for two days more in the place where He was."

Lazarus, laid in the tomb—and starting to corrupt—is a most vivid image of the spiritual experience of those who suffer this inward purification, apparently forgotten and abandoned by God.

## 2.

Jesus was somewhere beyond the Jordan. He received the sisters' message, "Please, Lord, your dear friend is ill," and to all appearances, ignored their humble plea. When questioned by the other disciples about Lazarus, Jesus replied: "Lazarus, our friend, has fallen asleep." Later He acknowledged the fact of his death to the disciples in these words: "Lazarus is dead, and for your sake I am glad that I was not there so that you may believe. Come now, let us go to him."

When Jesus finally arrived at Bethany, He was confronted with the actual situation to which He had allowed His friend to sink. He heard the prayer of Martha and saw the tears of Mary. Her tears caused His heart to melt and His eyes to stream with tears. His inmost being was shaken. At Pentecost the house where the disciples were gathered was shaken by a mighty wind. This shaking of Jesus' inmost being was also a mighty movement of the Spirit who was about to fill the soul of Lazarus, just as He was later to fill the house where the disciples were gathered.

Shaken by this deep emotion stirred up by the Spirit, Jesus made His way to the tomb. "It was a cave and a huge stone lay against the entrance. 'Remove the stone,' Jesus said.

" 'Master,' Martha, the dead man's sister, said to Him, 'his body stinks by this time. He has been dead four days.'" Her faith was beginning to waver. Jesus quickly came to Martha's rescue with this magnificent promise: "Did I not tell you that if you have faith, you will see the glory of God?" This glory is the fullness of salvation.

Those who were present managed to get the stone away from the front of the tomb. Then Jesus prayed to His Father. The sublime work of re-creating a human being requires the cooperation of the Source of all life. "Father, I thank you for listening to me. I know that you always hear me, but I said it for the sake of the people surrounding me that they might believe that you have really sent me."

Jesus experienced another powerful movement of the Spirit within Him, and called out with a mighty voice, foreshadowing His last great cry on Calvary: "Lazarus, come forth!"

Not, "Come out," but, "Come *forth*." Come forth from your old life, which is more like death, to a life that is brand new. While the bystanders watched, "he who had been dead four days staggered forth, wrapped hand and foot with winding cloths, and with a bandage around his face."

Jesus said to them, "Unwrap him and let him go!"

Everyone who has truly borne his own sinfulness has borne the sinfulness of everyone else, and the world is redeemed again through him. He has died the most important death, which is that of the false self. When his physical death comes, it will be, like Christ's, a redeeming death.

Everyone has a hard core self-centeredness. This is symbolized by the heavy stone which sealed Lazarus into his tomb. Once one has experienced the weight of this stone, it is impossible to judge other people any more. One realizes too intimately the crushing burden of weakness, ignorance, and sin, with which every member of the human race is struggling.

3.

Two points in the story of Lazarus need to be emphasized: the consequences of the prayer of Mary of Bethany and the consequences of Lazarus' illness and death. The power of the prayer of Mary of Bethany, whose tears moved Jesus to raise her brother after four days in the grave, is particularly striking, because it was precisely the raising of Lazarus that set in motion the events which led to Jesus' crucifixion, and thus to the redemption of the world. Martha went to Jesus and prayed; nothing happened. Mary went to Him saying the very same words, and He immediately came into the village and worked the miracle. The raising of Lazarus is what settled the Pharisees on the necessity of Jesus' death. All the events in the life of Our Lord are gathered up into the Church and preserved through the ages to be poured out again and again as one generation succeeds another. Christ lives in the here and now, especially in the Sacraments of the Church, where He shares with us the graces that are recorded in the Gospel. Jesus could have brought on His passion by other ways. But He chose to take the final step that would inevitably lead to His death and to the redemption of the world, through the prayers of this woman—not by the action of any of the apostles.

This fact has to be placed side by side with the consequences of Lazarus' illness and death. If he had not accepted death, he could not have been raised from the dead at the prayer of Mary of Bethany. Thus, the dying of Lazarus possessed the same significance and led to the same consequences as the prayer of Mary. Both are revelations of the way things happen in the divine economy of salvation.

The illness and death of Lazarus are reflected in the world today on an enormous scale. The modern world lies under a pervasive sense of anguish, of being abandoned by God, or at least of experiencing Him as absent. This sense of God's absence is characterized by the loss of a sense of value in life itself and the consequent loneliness, emptiness, and bewilderment which beset modern man. In the Western world we are living in what has been called the post-Christian era. One has only to read a book like Malcolm X's life story to realize what this means for countless numbers of people. Cultural changes keep occurring with such frequency and urgency that few people can integrate them into their own past experiences or into the traditions from which they come. Cut off from its roots and abandoned to what seem to be uncontrollable forces of political and social change, the modern world feels an increasing sense of doom descending upon it.

This experience is bound to be reflected in the Church. Christians will be called by God to enter into the agony of our time and to be willing to share, though in a redemptive manner, in the same psychological experience of alienation from God.

When Our Lord at the prayer of Mary raised Lazarus from the dead, many believed in Him. Such is the power of those who are willing to bear the consequences of sin at whatever historical time they may live. In our time, the consequences of sin are really colossal. As the sense of alienation from God in the world today is very deep, so also participation in this experience is bound to be very deep. Events that seem to turn our lives upside down and inside out are part of God's redemptive plan, not only for us, but for the world in which we live. God may be preparing a great awakening for the world, if He can find enough people like Lazarus and Mary to cooperate in His mysterious plan. Theirs is a special kind of poverty, a poverty so intense and so complete that no word can describe it except *death.*

### 4.

Lazarus is the image of the growing consciousness of one's sinfulness ending in the death of the false self. All the way to this tomb is a great grace; much more is coming out of it. All the way to this tomb is also challenging to faith. If one enjoyed the assurance that Our Lord was close, it would not be much of an illness or much of a death. To be really effective, one must feel the sense of God's absence; one's idea of God must be shattered. This is the major symptom of the illness. Lazarus, as a dead man, was not aware of all the action taking place outside the tomb. He did not know that there was a great crowd of mourners gathered there, and that Jesus had finally come, and just how close Jesus was to him now.

The darkness, dampness, lack of air in the burial chamber are all symbols of Lazarus' psychological state and inmost feelings. The great stone sealing the tomb signifies his sense of being hemmed in and imprisoned. What happens when the stone is rolled away?

Instantly a shaft of light dissipates the darkness. No

dawn is ever so welcome as after a night spent in absolute darkness. A wave of fresh air pours in, freeing the tomb from its suffocating stuffiness. Warmth enters the cave, drying up the damp walls, tempering the chill. Lazarus begins to feel some relief from the terrible sense of confinement. Hope breaks in upon him. His longing to be free increases. His love for God is enkindled. But it is only the beginning—the first stirring of divine Life as he begins to awaken from the stupor of spiritual death.

Now comes the strong cry of Jesus, which Lazarus heard in his inmost being—a sound that sent the walls of his inner prison crashing to the ground. To be called by name, as Mary Magdalen was,[6] is not so much to hear the voice of Christ with your ears, as to know in your inmost being, with invincible conviction, that God knows you inside and out—*everything*—and still loves you! That is the information which everyone is longing to hear and to have verified again and again! To be called by name takes place when God gives the interior assurance that He loves you. This knowledge penetrates to every part of your being, body, soul, and spirit.

Lazarus awakens to the full awareness of God's love for him, as the Holy Spirit is poured into his spirit by the strong voice of Jesus. He rises, leaving behind his cramped, inadequate, merely human way of looking at things. His first steps—because he was still bound hand and foot—could only be halting and stumbling. The awakening to divine Life does not normally take place in a single moment, but gradually.

He struggles to the mouth of the cave. His eyes meet those of Jesus. He waits there to receive the embrace of Him to whom he has already been inwardly united.

Lazarus' inner resurrection is not complete until the

crowning grace is bestowed upon him: "Unloose him and let him go!" He was standing at the mouth of the tomb, "wrapped hand and foot, his face muffled with a scarf."

What are we to understand by this unloosening? Freedom from all that death and the tomb stand for. His weakness is replaced by the virtues of Jesus Himself. His spirit is alive to every movement of the Spirit within him. He is led now, not by his own human spirit, but by the divine Spirit, who has taken possession of all his faculties.

Lazarus now enjoys the freedom to experience the fruits of the Spirit—charity, joy, peace. Freedom to savor that love which casts out all fear. Freedom to expand in boundless confidence in the Father. Freedom to celebrate the nuptial banquet of divine union, symbolized by his presence at the supper at Simon the Leper's house. Freedom to run the way of God's commandments. Freedom to be his true self, to be the person that God made him to be. Freedom from all the limitations of his environment, his early life, culture, education. Freedom from all his neurotic tendencies and all the effects of his sins. Freedom to leap and dance, and to celebrate the mystery of divine Life—and that perfectly human life, which is the divine Life in us.

[1]John 11:1-7
[2]Job 13:24-28
[3]Ps. 69:1-5
[4]Jonah 2:4-5
[5]Lam. 3:1-9
[6]John 20:11ff

# More Titles from St Bede's

**The Wheel of Becoming**: Personal Growth through the
Liturgical Year                                    *Augustin Belisle, OSB*

"The liturgical seasons celebrate the various mysteries of Christ. Since
Jesus is our model who has shown us the way to God, we consider Christ
to be the fullest expression of what it means to be human. Our celebrations of Christ through the year are really celebrations of human life at
its fullest," says the author. Reflecting on this seasonal cycle of the
liturgical year, Fr. Augustin presents insights into the rhythms and
seasons of everyone's journey through the mysteries of Christ, and
helps you to understand more clearly how these mysteries are directly
connected with your own growth as a human person. *Beautiful readings!*
**Paperback, 87 pages   ISBN 6-57-7**                            **$5.95**

**Hammer & Fire:**The Way to Contemplative Happiness, Fruitful
Ministry, and Mental Health            *Raphael Simon, OCSO, MD*
Many people today are seeking guidance, but are confused by the
various methods of spirituality being presented to them. This book
instructs us in the Gospel path of transformation in Christ through
prayer and meditation, in accordance with sound doctrine, scripture,
tradition, and the principles of mental health and personal development. Fr. Simon not only attempts to set up a program of spiritual
direction for the lay person, but also provides principles of direction for
priests, religious, and all who are called upon to counsel others. It is a
profound and very complete guide.
**Paperback, 268 pages   ISBN 6-52-6**                           **$9.95**

**Pathways of Spiritual Living**                      *Susan A. Muto*
Focusing on the universal call to holiness, acclaimed author Susan Muto
takes you through each step along the path of spiritual living: silence,
solitude, prayer, reading, meditation, journal-keeping, contemplation,
and service. She successfully harmonizes the wisdom of medieval spiritual masters with contemporary spiritual living in the midst of secular
pursuits. A thoroughly modern spiritual handbook for Christians "in
the world," it will be read and re-read for years to come.
**Paperback, 191 pages   ISBN 6-65-8**                          **$6.95**

**My Heart and I:** Interior Conversations, 1952-1959
*Catherine de Hueck Doherty*
Written in semi-diary form, the author shares with you her own deep, truly mystical reflections on the mystery of suffering, the relationship between herself and Christ, and other joys and sorrows in her life. A beautiful book; each entry deserves to be savored.
Paperback, 125 pages   ISBN 6-59-3                    **$5.95**

**The Steps of Love** In *The Dialogue* of St. Catherine of Siena
*Mary Ann Follmar (Dominican)*
*The Dialogue* of St. Catherine usually meets with a bewildered response from readers. As an aid to discovering the richness of this mystical treatise, the author introduces the spiritual journey outlined in *The Dialogue* and comments on the insights provided therein toward spiritual growth. Makes for fascinating reading!
Paperback, 84 pages   ISBN 6-17-8                    **$4.95**

**Spirituality Recharted**           *Hubert van Zeller*
In this delightful book, Dom Hubert discusses the pursuit of sanctity "by responding to the grace of spirituality," putting into everyday language St. John of the Cross' treatment of the soul's progress toward union with God.
Paperback, 157 pages   ISBN 6-39-9                    **$4.95**

**The Benedictine Way**           *Wulstan Mork, OSB*
Written as a commentary on the vows for monks and nuns, this little book is meant for all of us who are hungering for deeper prayer. Benedictine prayer is simple and direct, and this guide will take you back to the sources of Christian spirituality.
Paperback, 95 pages   ISBN 6-32-1                    **$5.95**

**The Holy Dybbuk:** Letters of Charles Rich
*ed. by Ronda Chervin*
This beautiful book of letters from Mr. Rich to his close spiritual friend, Ronda Chervin, is a journal of the interior experience of God shared between them. One of the strongest themes running through the letters is that of the way spiritual love in Christ is a foretaste of heaven, showing that even here on earth we can experience the joy of the union of persons which will be ours in eternity.
Paperback, 143 pages   ISBN 6-50-X                    **$7.50**

## A Padre Pio Profile
*Rev. John A. Schug, Cap.*

Interviews with several of Padre Pio's confreres, his doctors and spiritual directors, and with some of his spiritual children who received cures or special graces through his prayers. New or little-known information is brought out in these interviews concerning the Padre's fruitful spiritual life. The book ends with an up-to-date account of the canonization process being conducted for Padre Pio's cause.

Paperback, 163 pages    ISBN 6-56-9                               $6.95

## Teresa of Avila
*Marcelle Auclair*

At long last, this popular book returns to us! Reprinted with numerous up-to-date photos, this all-new edition is a *must* for Teresa of Avila fans. Marcelle Auclair recounts with wit and vividness of style, this best-loved saint's biography. Teresa comes to life and becomes a part of your life in this wonderful book. A spiritual classic.

Paperback, 454 pages    ISBN 6-67-4                              $12.95

## The Ingrafting: The Stories of Ten Hebrew-Catholics·
*ed. by Ronda Chervin*

Charles Rich, Fr. Raphael Simon, Ronda Chervin, and seven other Hebrew-Catholics recount the stories of their search for truth and their subsequent conversions to the Catholic faith. Told with charm and humor, these captivating stories reveal a depth of understanding as each author comes to see that Catholicism is actually the fulfillment of his or her own rich Jewish heritage.

Paperback, 117 pages    ISBN 6-55-0                               $6.95

## Gateway to Hope: An Exploration of Failure *Maria Boulding, OSB*

Learning to deal with failure is a part of life. Drawing on the Bible and on human experience, the author shows that in our failure lies our success. Weakness, sin, death itself have all been overcome, for in the ultimate failure—the Cross—we see the greatest triumph of both man and God: the gateway to our hope and to the glory that awaits us.

Paperback, 158 pages    ISBN 6-53-4                               $4.95

## On the Palm of His Hand
*Marion Lee Levandowski*

Everyone loves the story of an 11th-hour miracle, when God intervenes in human affairs to bring about a healing. But what about those who beg for a miracle, plead with God to spare a loved one, but whose words are seemingly ignored? Are their prayers heard? Does God care? This

beautiful story of the death of a close friend of the author shows just how much God does care and how he listens to all our prayers. It assures us that he is as present in death as in a miraculous cure. A moving memory of a journey of faith. Will be of special interest to prayer groups.
**Paperback, 85 pages    ISBN 6-62-3**                                        **$4.95**

**By Death Parted:** The Stories of Six Widows

*ed. by Dom Philip Jebb*

Whether you have faced the trials of widowhood or not, you will be charmed by these moving accounts written by six widows (of all ages) of their first years of widowhood, and how they learned to cope with the loneliness and the problems of being "suddenly single." The book offers spiritual consolation as well as practical advice for all who have been recently widowed. Makes a beautiful gift for a friend.
**Paperback, 101 pages    ISBN 6-45-3**                                       **$4.95**

**Widowed**                                                    *Dom Philip Jebb*

A best-seller both in England and in the USA! This sourcebook for the widowed touches on practical problems while developing a spirituality of widowhood, pointing out that the Church itself has been a widow since the ascension of Christ. Beautiful and moving!
**Paperback, 90 pages    ISBN 6-30-5**                                        **$2.95**

**Reflections**                                                  *Charles Rich*

A book of profound yet simple spiritual wisdom for all interested in personal growth in holiness. The author, a lay contemplative, leads you through various aspects of the spiritual life such as the meaning of suffering, the nature of prayer, and being one with Christ. This book will help you to focus on the ultimate reality—God.
**Paperback, 131 pages    ISBN 6-49-6**                                       **$5.95**

Available from your bookstore or:

**St Bede's Publications**
**PO Box 545, North Main Street**
**Petersham, MA 01366-0545**

**Please enclose $2.00 for the first book, 50¢ ea. additional book,**
**for shipping/handling charges. Thank you.**
**Send for our full catalog of books and tapes**